KIDS' FURNITURE
YOU CAN BUILD

THE WEEKEND PROJECT BOOK SERIES

Kids' Furniture You Can Build, by David & Jeanie Stiles
Playhouses You Can Build, by David & Jeanie Stiles

A WEEKEND PROJECT BOOK

KIDS' FURNITURE
YOU CAN BUILD

By David & Jeanie Stiles

CHAPTERS PUBLISHING LTD., SHELBURNE, VERMONT 05482

Published by Chapters Publishing Ltd.
2031 Shelburne Road
Shelburne, Vermont 05482

Library of Congress Cataloging-in-Publication Data

Stiles, David R.
    Kids furniture you can build / by David & Jeanie Stiles.
    p.   cm. — (The Weekend project book series.)
    Rev. ed. of: Easy-to-make children's furniture.
    ISBN 1-881527-49-2: $17.95
    1. Children's furniture. I. Stiles, Jeanie. II. Stiles, David R. Easy-to-make
children's furniture. III. Title. IV. Series.
TT197.5.C5S743   1994
684.1'04—dc20   94-29040

Trade distribution by Firefly Books Ltd.
250 Sparks Avenue
Willowdale, Ontario
Canada M2H 2S4

Printed and bound in Canada by Metropole Litho
St. Bruno de Montarville, Quebec

Designed by Eugenie Seidenberg Delaney
Photography by Gary Clayton-Hall

To our daughter
Lief-Anne

Acknowledgments

Many thanks to our editor Sandy Taylor,
copy editor John Matthews and designer Eugenie Delaney
for their guidance and support.

CONTENTS

FIRST STEPS

INTRODUCTION

This book was inspired by our frustration with the children's furniture and equipment available on the market. We had just had a baby girl and had bought a new crib. Besides delivering the crib late and dented, the retail store neglected to include the instructions for assembly. Out of the carton dropped an assortment of rods, screws, nuts, bolts, washers and springs, all of which seemed to be of mysteriously inconsistent sizes. "Have no fear," said Jeanie. "David is an industrial designer and will have this thing together in no time!" Three hours later, with sweat pouring off David's forehead and after having used every swear word he knows, this industrial designer finally finished assembling the crib. It seemed that every logical guess he had made turned out to be wrong — particularly since the functions of the rods and springs were never explained. Only when David was finished did he understand how the crib worked. This was a valuable lesson for us, and one we kept in the back of our minds when designing the projects in this book.

A majority of books on do-it-yourself projects are written by professionals whose knowledge, skills and equipment far exceed those of the amateur. This book is written by people like you. We assumed our readers would have some hands-on experience working with both manual and electric tools but — like many of us — they wouldn't have a great deal of time, money or tools to devote to projects. On the other hand, when you invest your time and effort to make something for your children, you want the finished product to be something you can be proud of, something your child will enjoy, something that will be lasting.

We have attempted to make the instructions and drawings in this book as understandable as possible. To ensure that the instructions we've given are sound, we have built every project our-selves. Whenever possible, we've tested the project with a child (usually our own) and have made modifications if necessary.

DESIGN

You may notice that most of the furniture shown here shares a common look. Rather than attempting to create a new style in the kids' furniture market, our designs simply evolved by following a few commonsense requirements.

The first requirement was that the piece be *safe*. Consequently, wherever possible we have recommended that you round off all corners and edges to prevent injury to the child. This may seem obvious, but very few if any children's furniture manufacturers have incorporated this feature into their lines. Unfortunately, you'll find when making these projects that it's practically impossible to cut plywood without creating a splintered edge. This problem is neatly solved by rounding off the edge with a four-in-hand (or rasp) and sandpaper (see page 26 for instructions).

The second requirement was that all the projects be easy to make with a minimum number of tools. Although some tasks are simpler with an electric router, we have provided alternative solutions, as with making drawers (pages 28-33).

The third requirement was that all the pieces of furniture be easy to clean. Therefore, we recommend either painting the wooden surfaces with polyurethane or enamel paint (see page 27) or using melamine board, which cleans like Formica.

The fourth requirement was that, whenever possible, the piece could be easily made into something useful after it had outlived its original purpose. For example, the crib can be converted into a child-sized couch. Convertibility helps to minimize the built-in obsolescence factor of manufactured children's furniture.

A Word about Safety

Much care was taken to ensure the safety of the projects for children. In most cases we exceeded the guidelines set forth by the U.S. Consumer Product Safety Commission. Coatings were checked for toxicity, edges were rounded and hinges were redesigned to eliminate possible scissoring action. It is important to follow the directions carefully, to eliminate wood splinters by sanding and sealing and to use common sense where unusual conditions exist.

In regard to your own safety, remember that all tools — both manual and power — can be dangerous if handled carelessly. It is important to exercise extreme caution at all times and to keep *all* tools out of the reach of children. Note that any time you use a power tool you should always check before starting to see that the electrical cord is behind you or off to one side so that you don't cut through it.

Tools You Will Need

To build most of the projects in this book you'll need only the most basic tools, which we listed below in their rough order of importance.

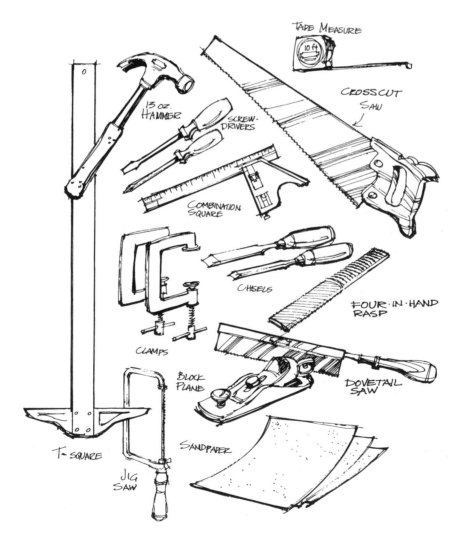

Fig. 1-1

HAND TOOLS

Hammer: a 13- or 14-ounce claw hammer

Screwdrivers: one medium-sized flathead type and one Phillips-head type

Crosscut Saw: 6 to 8 teeth (points) per inch

Tape Measure: ½ inch wide, at least 8 feet long, locking mechanism

Combination Square: with 45-degree angle

Framing Square

T-square: 48 inches long with 1-inch increments

Clamps: two C-clamps are best

Wood Chisels: ¼ inch and ¾ inch wide

Rasp/File Combination: sometimes called a four-in-hand or shoe rasp

Jig Saw or Coping Saw: for cutting rounded corners

Dovetail Saw: 1 small 18-inch backsaw for small grooves and joints

Miter Box and Backsaw: You can make all the mitered (45-degree angle) cuts freehand. However, for a more professional job, use a miter box (see page 58, Fig. 2-11). This handy, inexpensive jig sits on the edge of your workbench and guides your saw blade at 45- or 90-degree angles, helping you to make perfect cuts. Although it is best to use a stiff backsaw, a "standard" crosscut handsaw works also. Make sure the wood you are cutting is pressed against the back wall of the miter box (using your free hand) and that you cut on the waste side of the marked line.

Nail Set

Compass

Block Plane: 6 inches long, used for trimming

Carbide Scoring Knife

Spackle Knife

ELECTRIC TOOLS

Drill: ⅜-inch chuck, variable-speed reversible, with flat (spade) wood drill bits in sizes ¼, ⅜, ½, ⅝, ¾ and 1 inch. Buy the bits as you need them. Although a good electric drill can be a somewhat

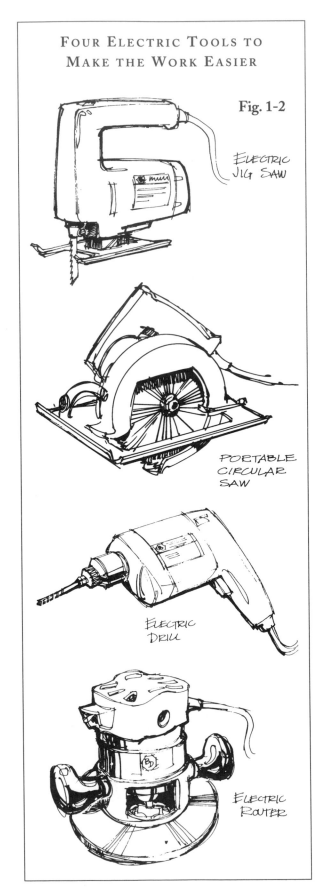

FOUR ELECTRIC TOOLS TO MAKE THE WORK EASIER

Fig. 1-2

ELECTRIC JIG SAW

PORTABLE CIRCULAR SAW

ELECTRIC DRILL

ELECTRIC ROUTER

expensive item, according to a recent survey electric tools have not kept up with inflation over the past twenty years and are a good investment. A good drill should last ten to twenty years. An electric drill is an indispensable tool to have around the house, even for the novice woodworker. It is also one of the safest electric tools you can own. Variable speeds are a nice feature, especially for beginners.

Jig or Saber Saw: Although most of the projects in this book can be made with a handsaw, you will save a lot of time and effort by using an electric jig saw (not to be confused with a reciprocating saw). It pays to buy a more expensive make since they will last much longer than cheaper brands.

Router: It is not essential that you use an electric router when building most of the projects in this book, but it is helpful if you want to make professional dadoes (grooves) or rabbets (shoulder cuts), with examples of both being shown in Fig. 1-3. The nice thing about a router is that it works quickly and makes a clean, sharp cut that rarely requires additional sanding. Routers are relatively

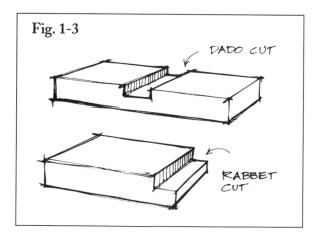

Fig. 1-3

DADO CUT

RABBET CUT

safe as long as you use them according to the directions, but be prepared for a loud noise.

If you plan to make five or more projects for which a router is suggested, you should consider buying one even before investing in a table saw with a dado head. Be forewarned that in addition to the router you must also buy three or four

router bits, and this quantity can cost as much as the router itself. If you are cutting birch plywood you must use carbide bits, which are expensive but save money in the long run. In place of a router you can buy a simple dovetail saw or backsaw and use it for your dado and rabbet cuts (see page 11, Fig. 1-1).

Portable Circular Saw: An electric portable circular saw (sometimes referred to as a skilsaw) is a useful and popular tool to own. It can save much cutting time but must be used with caution. In order to avoid sudden bucking or kickback from the saw, make sure to position your lumber so that the waste piece falls away from the saw blade (see page 21, Fig. 1-8).

HOW TO AVOID ERRORS

Mistakes can be minimized by following a few basic rules:

1. Before cutting any wood, study the plans carefully and be sure you understand them. If you want to change the plans, make a scale drawing at 1 inch to the foot indicating the change.

2. Check and double-check any extenuating circumstances that might affect the design of a project, such as whether it will fit through the doorway of the room it is going in, whether it's the right size for your child and whether the project requires an expensive tool that you don't own.

3. Don't take anything for granted. When buying wood, check for warping, knots, dents and cracks. Also measure the thickness. You may think you've bought a ¾-inch-thick piece of plywood and find, as I did on one occasion, that it's actually ¹⁄₁₆ inch thinner! Even stock lumber like 2x4s can vary from lumber mill to lumber mill. If the wood seems inordinately heavy to you it may be because it has not been seasoned (dried) long enough, which could cause warpage later.

4. Measure things more than once to ensure

accuracy. When measuring for a long cut, make sure you mark four or five times across the length of the board with a pencil and connect these marks with a line drawn using a very straight board as a straightedge. It's a good idea to set aside a straight 1x4 specifically for this purpose.

5. Don't try to read your tape measure upside down. The numbers *6* and *9* can be mistaken for *9* and *6*. Before cutting each piece, try to visualize how the piece will connect to others. Ask yourself if the size of the piece you are about to cut makes sense.

6. Wherever and whenever possible, don't rely on transferring measurements by using a ruler. For instance, if you need to cut four identical pieces of wood, use the first piece as a template for the next three, minus a pencil-line thickness.

7. Always keep the kerf (the width of the cut) in mind. For example, an electric portable circular saw removes about ⅛ inch of material when making a cut. Consequently, you should cut to the waste side of your layout line while cutting when your dimensions allow. When this isn't possible, make the cut so that the kerf is divided equally on either side of the layout line.

MATERIALS
BOARD OR DIMENSION LUMBER

Lumberyards and home-improvement centers stock various sizes and types of board lumber that come in basically two grades: clear and #2 construction. If you are going to paint your child's furniture, there is no reason why you shouldn't choose the more economical #2 construction lumber. It is, however, a good idea to paint the knots with a shellac-based sealer in order to prevent them from staining through the lighter colors of paint. If you choose clear (knot-free lumber), expect to pay dearly. An 8-foot

clear white pine 1x6 costs as much as a bottle of champagne! In either case, always check each piece for warping by looking down the edge from the end of the board.

Most ¾-inch-thick lumber (referred to as 1-inch-thick lumber by the lumberyard) comes in the following sizes:

REFERENCE (Nominal Size)	APPROXIMATE (Actual Size)
1x2s	¾ inch by 1½ inches
1x3s	¾ inch by 2½ inches
1x4s	¾ inch by 3½ inches
1x6s	¾ inch by 5½ inches
1x8s	¾ inch by 7¼ inches
1x10s	¾ inch by 9¼ inches
1x12s	¾ inch by 11¼ inches

Likewise, 2x lumber has similar reference and actual sizes. Most 2x lumber is actually 1½ inches thick.

PLYWOOD

Since most of the projects in this book are made with plywood, you should familiarize yourself with the various kinds that are available. Plywood is made up of several layers of thin wood sandwiched together so that the grain of adjacent layers is perpendicular (at right angles). The most common plywood is fir plywood, which has a "swirled" raised grain and is not as desirable as lauan plywood, which has a more consistently straight grain.

Plywood is generally sold in 4x8 sheets in ¼-, ⅜-, ½-, ⅝- and ¾-inch thicknesses; however, many lumberyards and home centers (and more frequently hardware stores) are now carrying it in 4x4 half sheets.

Plywood also comes in various grades, but there are two to keep in mind:

A/A sheets have no blemishes on either side.

A/D sheets have one good side and one bad

side. A/D plywood is an acceptable choice and much cheaper than solid white pine.

Most plywoods have voids or spaces inside that are visible on the edges when you cut through the wood. They can be filled in, however, with wood putty.

A good alternative to fir plywood is a relatively new type of material called MDO (medium-density overlay), which was originally developed for exterior signs. A paper-faced plywood, it is more waterproof than uncoated plywood and its surface is excellent for painting. It can be special-ordered at most home centers and lumberyards and is quite expensive.

For a really beautiful job, use birch veneer (cabinet quality) plywood. Most of the projects in this book were made with birch veneer plywood, which is more expensive than fir. It also has a good and a bad side, so be sure to leave the good side exposed and to protect the good side from nicks and scratches.

Another choice of material is called lumber core, which has solid wood inside instead of thin layers of wood. However, for the highest quality plywood, ask your lumber dealer to special-order thirteen-ply Baltic plywood; it is generally not stocked in most lumberyards. Most of this plywood is shipped from Europe and is expensive.

Cutting Plywood

There are several ways to cut plywood, depending on your skill, experience and tools. All of these techniques can also be used to cut MDO, particleboard or melamine.

Precutting at the Lumberyard

The easiest way to cut up a sheet of plywood is to have the lumberyard do it for you. Most lumberyards offer this service and will charge you either a flat rate per sheet or by the hour.

They often have a vertical wall-mounted saw that enables them to cut a sheet of plywood in just a few minutes. The disadvantage is that they will not guarantee accuracy of under ⅛ inch, but you can usually compensate for this when you build. You must be absolutely sure of your dimensions before the wood is cut and give the lumberyard an accurate sketch of the cuts, called the cutting plan. This should be drawn to scale with a ruler using a 1 inch to the foot scale. You must allow for the kerf (material taken away by the saw blade itself — usually ⅛ inch) and indicate scrap by crosshatching (see Fig. 1-4). To figure out the

Fig. 1-4

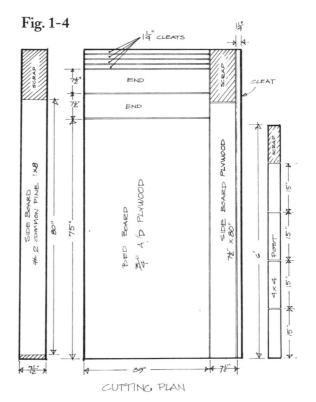

CUTTING PLAN

most economical way of laying out the sheet for cutting, you may want to cut the pieces to scale out of paper and rearrange them on a piece of paper representing a 4x8 sheet.

The advantages of having the lumberyard cut the wood are that all the pieces will have nice right-angle edges, you will have saved yourself an hour or more of work and you will have eliminated the nuisance of getting sawdust over every-

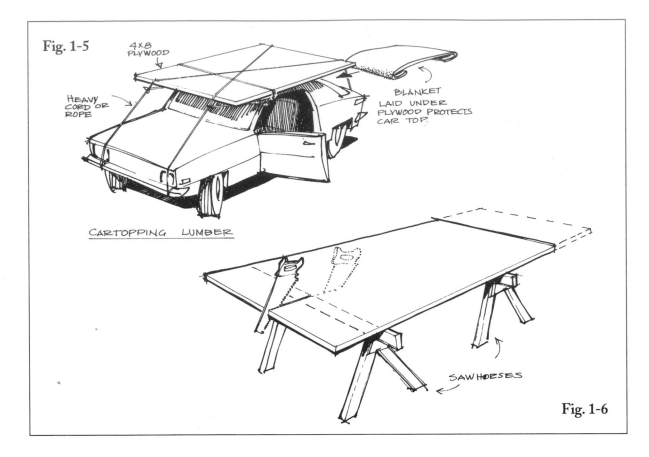

Fig. 1-5

4×8 PLYWOOD

HEAVY CORD OR ROPE

BLANKET LAID UNDER PLYWOOD PROTECTS CAR TOP.

CARTOPPING LUMBER

SAWHORSES

Fig. 1-6

thing. To keep things orderly, write the dimensions and description of each piece on tape and ask the cutter at the lumberyard to attach the tape to the corresponding piece after it is cut. Since lumberyards can (and often do) make mistakes, be sure to check the measurements of each piece before you leave.

If you buy the plywood uncut, there is the problem of getting one or more heavy 4x8 sheets of plywood home. Many lumberyards will deliver for free with a minimum order — sometimes over $75. So you have to either pay for delivery or, if you have a car, pick it up yourself. A 4x8 sheet of plywood won't fit inside most cars, but it can be carried on the roof. Bring along an old blanket to keep from scratching the car and use lots of heavy hemp cord to secure the plywood to the roof, crisscrossing it over the top of the car (see Fig. 1-5). Be sure to tie the plywood so it can't shift forward should you have to suddenly apply your brakes.

HANDSAWING PLYWOOD

If you prefer to cut the plywood by hand, here are some tips to make the job easier:

Make sure your saw is sharp. The saw teeth should feel sharp to the touch. If they are not, take your saw to the hardware store or lumberyard and have it sharpened. This is generally an inexpensive service.

The most overlooked aspect of sawing a piece of plywood is how to support the wood while you're cutting it. A handsaw requires about 1 foot of clearance under the cut for the saw blade, which means you must support the plywood on something rather tall while you are sawing.

If you have two sawhorses (see Fig. 1-6), you can start the cut at the far end and, as you get closer to the front sawhorse, shift the plywood so the saw is in between the two. Continue cutting toward the back sawhorse and then shift the

FOOTSTOOL, PAGE 50

PORTABLE FOLDING TABLE, PAGE 53

LOFT BED, PAGE 74

STORAGE CHAIR, PAGE 95 AND ADJUST-TABLE, PAGE 90

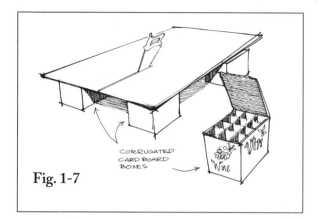

Fig. 1-7

CORRUGATED
CARD BOARD
BOXES

sheet of plywood again.

If you don't have sawhorses, you can use four sturdy chairs of equal height. Plastic milk cartons are very handy and even corrugated cardboard liquor boxes will do (see Fig. 1-7). Leave any dividers in the boxes, stand the boxes upright and position them so the plywood will not fall inward when it is cut through.

Place the plywood on the supporting structure so that the good side is facing upward. To start cutting, rest the saw on the far top edge of the plywood and make several short pulls toward you. It is best to start this way because the teeth are facing slightly forward, which makes it difficult to start with a forward stroke. Make enough backstrokes to get a good start into the wood and then alternately push and pull the following strokes. Keep your eye on the blade to be sure the saw is vertical. Make long, even strokes, keeping your wrist as stiff as possible. Remember, only the forward stroke is doing the cutting. If you are cutting a small piece of wood, use two clamps to secure it to a stationary surface while cutting.

CUTTING PLYWOOD WITH A PORTABLE CIRCULAR SAW

Fig. 1-8

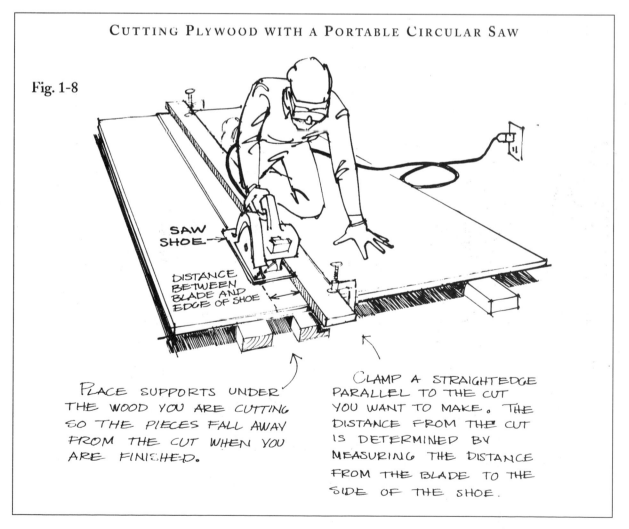

SAW SHOE

DISTANCE BETWEEN BLADE AND EDGE OF SHOE

PLACE SUPPORTS UNDER THE WOOD YOU ARE CUTTING SO THE PIECES FALL AWAY FROM THE CUT WHEN YOU ARE FINISHED.

CLAMP A STRAIGHTEDGE PARALLEL TO THE CUT YOU WANT TO MAKE. THE DISTANCE FROM THE CUT IS DETERMINED BY MEASURING THE DISTANCE FROM THE BLADE TO THE SIDE OF THE SHOE.

CUTTING PLYWOOD WITH A PORTABLE CIRCULAR SAW

First of all, always remember to keep the width of the cut in mind (see Step 7, page 14). Place the good side of the plywood so it is facing downward (face up when using a table saw). Make sure the piece you are sawing off is supported on the same level as the original piece. Position the supports under the plywood so the pieces fall away from the cut when you finish cutting the panel (see Fig. 1-8). It is always a good idea to wear ear and eye protection when cutting.

Always keep a long, straight piece of 1x6 handy for use as a straightedge when you want to make long straight cuts (also called ripping). Clamp the two ends of the straightedge to the plywood parallel to the cut. The distance from the cut is determined by measuring the distance from the blade to the side of the saw shoe. You may, in fact, prefer to have two 1x6 straightedges: an 8-foot-long piece for ripping and a 4-foot-long piece for crosscutting.

ALTERNATIVES TO PLYWOOD

Particleboard, also called industrial flakeboard, is a good alternative to plywood and costs about half the price of A/D fir plywood. Also sold in 4x8 sheets, it is very flat and stable. It is used extensively for furniture and kitchen cabinets.

Particleboard's disadvantages are that it is somewhat heavy and cannot be nailed unless pilot holes are first drilled into the board. It is denser and is easier to paint than plywood. Remember to wear goggles to protect your eyes when cutting particleboard.

Another type of particleboard is sold under the name of melamine. This material, available in most lumberyards, has a very durable, hard and Formica-like surface on both sides. The surfaces of the particleboard are actually coated with white or wood-colored melamine.

Melamine is an excellent choice for building children's furniture not only because of its hard surface but also because it costs much less per sheet than birch veneer plywood. The edge of the particleboard can be filled with a sealer such as vinyl spackle. The edge can also be covered with melamine edging (also called edgebanding) tape, which is a preglued iron-on tape sold in ¾-inch-wide and 25-foot-long rolls. The heat from an iron liquifies the glue and causes the tape to adhere to the edges (see Fig. 1-11). When using this tape, do not round off the edges of the particleboard.

When melamine is cut with a handsaw, the edges of the surface coating tend to chip; therefore, if you are not covering the edges with edging tape, round them off and sand until smooth using a medium-grade sandpaper (see pages 26 and 27).

Since melamine's surface is nonporous, it should not be glued before preliminary steps are taken to ensure a good bond. Mark the surface where the glue will go and score or rough up the area using a carbide scoring knife (see Fig. 1-9). Try to make deep scratches so that the porous particleboard underneath the melamine surface is exposed.

After scoring the surface, predrill ³⁄₃₂-inch nail holes through the face of the melamine particleboard that you are joining to the edge of another piece.

Apply a generous amount of carpenter's glue to the porous edge of the adjoining piece of melamine particleboard and nail the two pieces together using 1⅝-inch annular (ringed) white panel nails (see Fig. 1-10). The heads of the nails will be slightly visible, but this can be corrected by countersinking the nails, using a nail set and filling the holes with vinyl spackle.

HOW TO WORK WITH MELAMINE

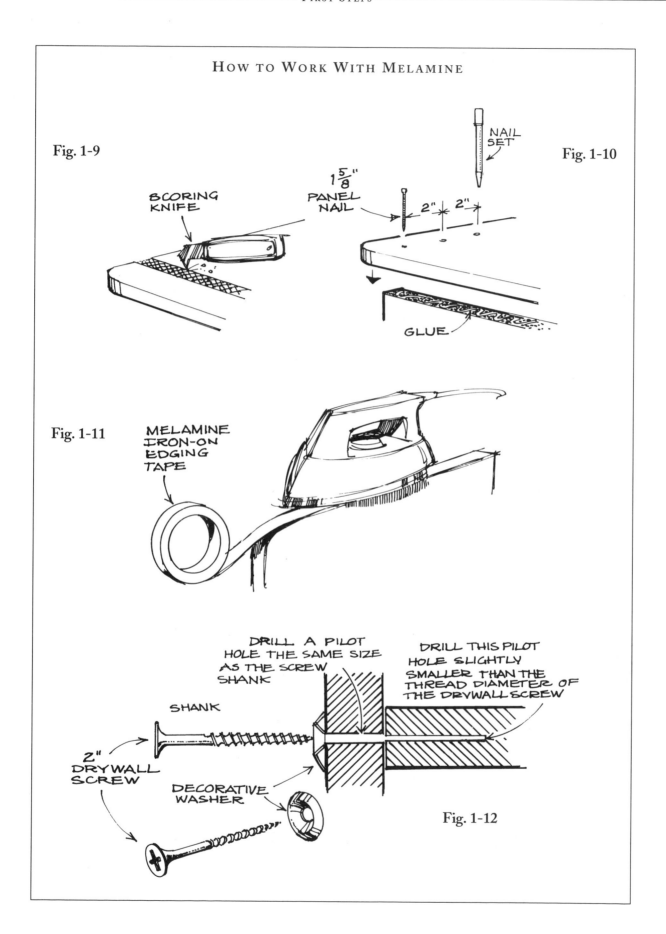

Fig. 1-9

SCORING
KNIFE

NAIL
SET

Fig. 1-10

$1\frac{5}{8}$" PANEL NAIL

2" 2"

GLUE

Fig. 1-11

MELAMINE
IRON-ON
EDGING
TAPE

DRILL A PILOT
HOLE THE SAME SIZE
AS THE SCREW
SHANK

DRILL THIS PILOT
HOLE SLIGHTLY
SMALLER THAN THE
THREAD DIAMETER OF
THE DRYWALL SCREW

SHANK

2"
DRYWALL
SCREW

DECORATIVE
WASHER

Fig. 1-12

Other tips for working with melamine:

1. Since some chipping may occur, saw blade teeth should enter the cut on the side of the panel that will be seen the most.

2. Melamine can be painted with oil-based paints, but you must first sand the surface with #120 sandpaper.

3. Melamine panels can be screwed together using drywall screws and stainless steel decorative washers, which is advantageous if you plan on disassembling the piece of furniture in the future. Be sure, however, to first drill pilot holes in both panels before driving the screws (see Fig. 1-12).

Hardboard (masonite) is a compressed wood-fiber panel sold in 4x8 sheets of ⅛ and ¼ inch thicknesses. Generally used for the bottoms of drawers or the backs of cabinets, it comes in two grades: tempered and nontempered. The tempered grade is dark brown, smooth and very hard. Pilot holes must be drilled into it before hammering in nails. The nontempered grade is light brown and not as hard, so making pilot holes before nailing isn't necessary.

FASTENERS

Most of the projects in this book require some sort of fasteners to hold the pieces of wood together in addition to glue. If you are joining plywood to plywood, 1½- to 2-inch finishing nails are recommended. When joining melamine or particleboard to another piece of melamine or particleboard, however, you should use a thinner nail, such as panel nails, that have annular rings and will grip the wood without splitting it.

Drywall screws have become very popular in building children's furniture since they provide a stronger joint and can be easily removed if a mistake is made. These require a Phillips-head screwdriver. (I prefer electric, reversible variable-speed screwdrivers or electric drills to manual screwdrivers.)

When trying to create very strong joints, use bolts as they are five times stronger than nails or screws and can be tightened if the wood shrinks. Bolts are also removable, which comes in handy when you move.

To help you identify the different types of fasteners (nails, screws, brads and bolts) when buying your supplies, please refer to Fig. 1-13.

GLUE

All the projects in this book are designed to be built using yellow carpenter's glue, which is water resistant and easy to use. If you plan to finish the piece of furniture in clear polyurethane or stain, be careful not to get glue on the surface of the wood or plywood as it will leave a mark. Have a moist sponge handy when you are gluing and assembling the pieces so that you can wipe up any drips immediately before the glue begins to dry.

After applying the glue to a piece of lumber, position its mate in place and then remove it to see if the glue has transferred to the second piece. If it has not transferred, apply more glue to the bare spots and reposition the pieces. Clamp or nail together.

WOOD PUTTY

The wood putty that is most commonly known is plastic wood; however, there are other types that are just as good, like wood dough and water putty.

Use wood putty to fill in the shallow holes that are left after countersinking finished nails or screws. After it dries (in about 15 to 20 minutes) sand it down so it is flush with the surface of the wood.

NAILS, SCREWS, BRADS AND BOLTS

Fig. 1-13

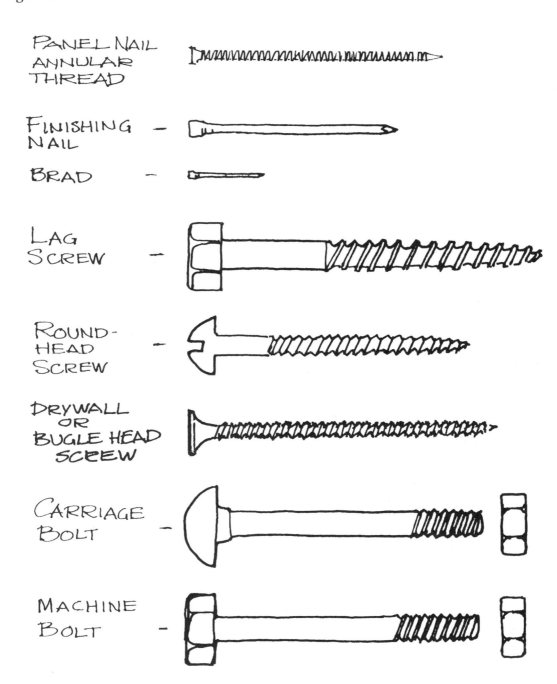

TRIMMING THE EDGES

Trimming or rounding off the edge of manufactured wood products like particleboard and plywood is no problem if you have an electric router. Simply insert a carbide rounding bit in the chuck of the router, set the depth and round off the plywood in one operation (see Fig. 1-14).

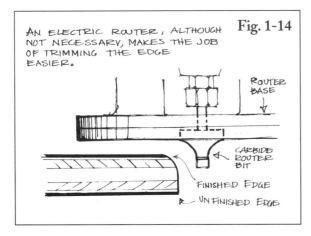

Fig. 1-14

AN ELECTRIC ROUTER, ALTHOUGH NOT NECESSARY, MAKES THE JOB OF TRIMMING THE EDGE EASIER.

ROUTER BASE

CARBIDE ROUTER BIT

FINISHED EDGE

UNFINISHED EDGE

If you don't own a router, you can still do a professional job by following these steps:

1. Clamp the piece securely to a bench. With a rasp or four-in-hand, file the edge down. Always stroke away from the edge, not into it (see Fig. 1-15).

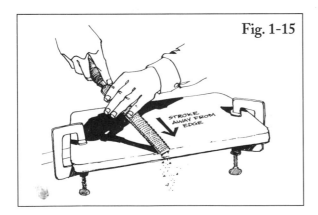

Fig. 1-15

STROKE AWAY FROM EDGE

2. Using a very small amount of contact cement, glue a coarse #50 piece of sandpaper to a 12-inch-long scrap of 1x4. This sanding block is one of the best and least expensive tools you'll

need for all the projects in this book, and it enables you to do a highly professional job.

Hold the block lengthwise to the work and make long strokes back and forth (see Fig. 1-16). In a very short time you will see the edge become rounded. Switch to a medium-grade #80 sandpaper and continue sanding until smooth.

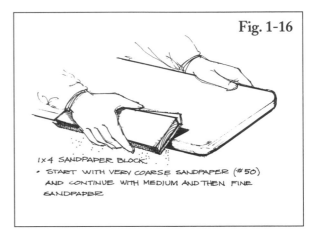

Fig. 1-16

1x4 SANDPAPER BLOCK.
• START WITH VERY COARSE SANDPAPER (#50) AND CONTINUE WITH MEDIUM AND THEN FINE SANDPAPER

3. Mark the corners to their required radius with a compass, cut them off with an electric jig saw and then file and sand the corners in the same way so that the curve (Fig. 1-17) blends into the straightedge. Finish sanding with a fine-grade #120 sandpaper. When the project is completely built, give the edges three coats of polyurethane or paint.

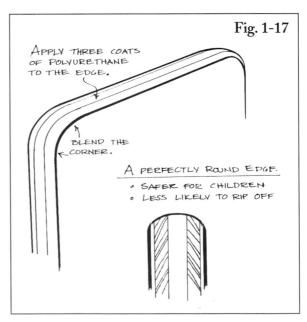

Fig. 1-17

APPLY THREE COATS OF POLYURETHANE TO THE EDGE.

BLEND THE CORNER.

A PERFECTLY ROUND EDGE.
• SAFER FOR CHILDREN
• LESS LIKELY TO RIP OFF

SANDPAPER

If you think all sandpaper is the same, you probably haven't tried garnet sandpaper — the same kind used on most emery boards. It is a reddish color, lasts at least five times longer than other kinds of sandpaper but it costs the same as other types. It is often impossible to find in hardware stores but can be ordered from the Woodworkers' Store (see Sources). Ask for garnet sandpaper made either by 3M or Carborundum. It comes in the following grades:

P2503	#120	Fine
P2505	#80	Medium
P2508	#50	Coarse

You will need more coarse-grade sheets than fine-grade sheets.

FINISHING SURFACES

Most of the projects in this book will require a finish of some kind — either clear or colored. If you are using birch plywood, it would be a shame to paint over the beautiful wood grain. It makes more sense instead to cover the birch with three coats of polyurethane. On the other hand, fir plywood, MDO or particleboard can all be enhanced with a sparkling coat of brightly colored enamel paint, and MDO needs no preparation. You can simply brush on two coats of enamel paint.

Other substances, however, are not as simple. Any good painter will tell you that the key to a professional paint job is in the preparation. If you are using fir plywood to build your children's furniture, you will see the swirly grain showing through the finished coat of paint unless you take the following steps in your preparation:

1. Using a block of coarse sandpaper (see Fig. 1-16), sand the flat surfaces lightly to remove any high spots.

2. Use a damp (not wet) sponge to moisten the surface of the plywood so it accepts the spackle more readily and removes dust from the sanding.

3. Using a 4-inch-wide spackle knife, cover the surface of the wood with vinyl spackle.

4. Fill any spaces or voids in the edges with wood putty.

5. When dry (approximately 30 minutes), sand all surfaces using a medium-grade sandpaper until they feel flat and smooth.

6. Spray or roll on a white, pigmented and shellac-based primer/sealer, such as BIN by Zinsser and allow to dry for approximately 15 minutes.

7. Sand the sealer lightly using a waterproof (also called wet/dry) sandpaper and a little water. Wipe with a clean towel when finished.

PAINTING SURFACES

Whether you use plywood that you have sealed, particleboard or MDO, you will probably want to paint your children's furniture a brilliant color. A latex paint is easy to clean up after and takes a minimal amount of time to dry between coats; however, for a more durable and longer lasting finish, we recommend using oil-based enamel paints. You can buy enamel paint in spray containers, but because of the likelihood of overspraying, it is better to buy a can of paint and brush it on. Cans also give you a wider range of colors to pick from and the option to custom-mix colors to achieve a particular shade. Use a small disposable 3-inch roller for each color, and keep it sealed securely in plastic wrap while the coats of paint dry. Sand any drips off the edges and cover them with three coats of polyurethane. Or, if you prefer, paint the edges.

DRAWERS AND SHELVES

Drawers are the most difficult part of any carpentry job. Great skill is required to measure and cut them to tolerances of ¹⁄₁₆ inch. The secret lies in making sure that the drawer and the cabinet it fits into are absolutely square *in all directions*. A professional cabinetmaker checks for squareness before, during and after each operation.

There are three main points to consider when making a drawer:

1. You must decide if the face of the drawer will fit flush with (see Fig. 1-18), inside of (see Fig. 1-19) or overlap (see Fig. 1-20) the front edges of the cabinet. The drawer that fits flush must be a perfect fit, with a consistent ¹⁄₁₆-inch crack showing between the drawer front and the front edges of the cabinet. This can sometimes be quite difficult, especially if you have several drawers. One way to avoid this problem is to indent or recess the drawer ½ inch so that the drawer purposely does not line up with the front edges of the cabinet (see Fig. 1-19). In this type of construction the face edge of the cabinet (labeled in Fig. 1-20) must be finished off in some special way.

Another solution is to construct drawers with fronts that overlap the front of the cabinet. You then need to finish off the side edges of the drawer, which will show (although not as much as on the front). This type of drawer provides a better air seal because it overlaps and touches the front edge of the cabinet (see Fig. 1-20).

2. Measure the space the drawer will occupy from side to side, front to back and top to bottom. If the drawer is small (under 4 inches high and 16 inches wide) it is advisable to use ½-inch clear pine for the sides, back and front. If the drawer is medium sized (6 inches high and 24 inches wide), it is advisable to use ½-inch plywood. If the drawer is much larger, use ⅝-inch or

DRAWERS—THREE TYPES OF DRAWER CONFIGURATIONS

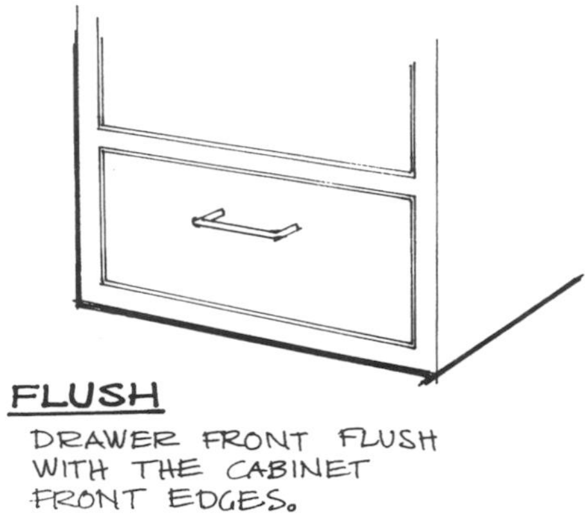

FLUSH
DRAWER FRONT FLUSH WITH THE CABINET FRONT EDGES.

Fig. 1-18

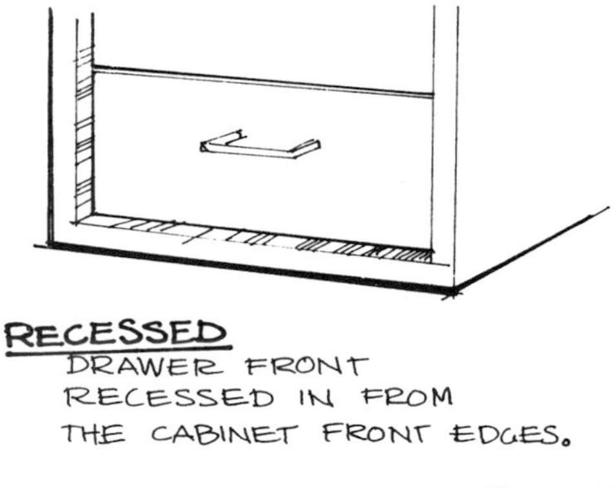

RECESSED
DRAWER FRONT RECESSED IN FROM THE CABINET FRONT EDGES.

Fig. 1-19

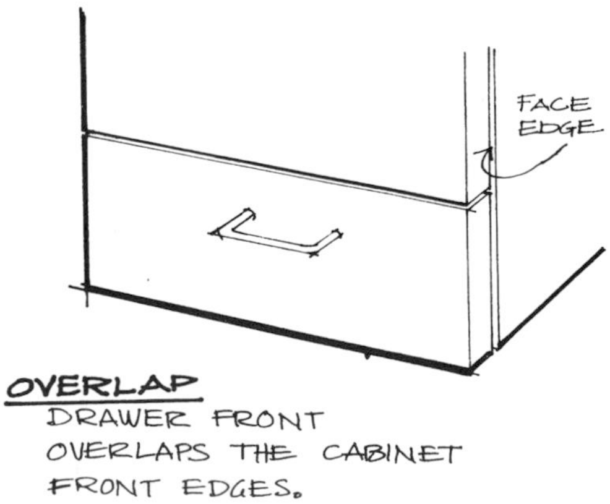

FACE EDGE

OVERLAP
DRAWER FRONT OVERLAPS THE CABINET FRONT EDGES.

Fig. 1-20

¾-inch plywood.

3. When planning your drawer, decide beforehand how it will be supported and by what means it will slide in and out. There are many ways to do this. The simplest is to cut a dado with a router or table saw into the side of each drawer from front to back and to attach cleats the same length as the dadoes but slightly thinner onto each side of the cabinet. The drawer slides on the two runners and requires only a ¹⁄₁₆-inch clearance on either side of the drawer.

This type of drawer slide works well if the drawer is small, since a ¼-inch-deep groove can be cut in the drawer sides using a router. If you don't have a router you can make the slide by nailing two strips of ¼-inch by ¾-inch wood cleats onto each side of the drawer and attaching another similar strip to the inside of the cabinet (see Fig. 1-21). Remember, you must allow at

least ¼ inch on each side between the drawer and the side of the cabinet to compensate for the thickness of the cleats plus another ¹⁄₁₆ inch on each side for general clearance.

Drawers that are made with lap joints rather than more professional-looking dadoes are perfectly all right as long as they are well glued. Lap joints take less time to make but will only last about fifty years, whereas dadoes will last over a century.

SIMPLE FLUSH LAP-JOINT DRAWER

Here is a way to make a small or medium-sized drawer using only a handsaw, a hammer and a square.

1. Cut all pieces from ½-inch-thick stock. Measure the cabinet opening and cut the face of

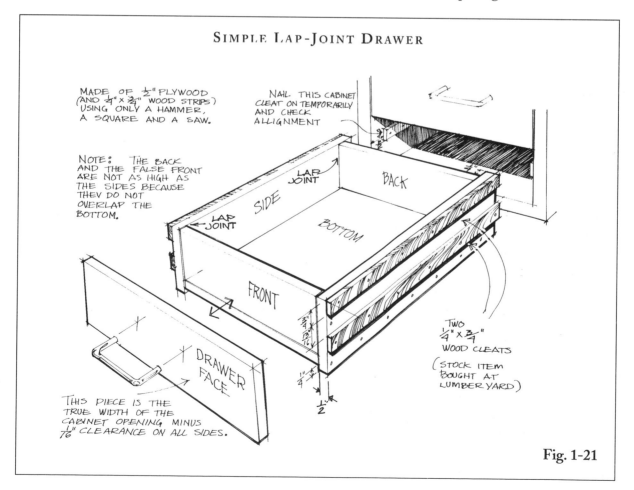

SIMPLE LAP-JOINT DRAWER

MADE OF ½" PLYWOOD (AND ¼" x ¾" WOOD STRIPS) USING ONLY A HAMMER, A SQUARE AND A SAW.

NAIL THIS CABINET CLEAT ON TEMPORARILY AND CHECK ALLIGNMENT

NOTE: THE BACK AND THE FALSE FRONT ARE NOT AS HIGH AS THE SIDES BECAUSE THEY DO NOT OVERLAP THE BOTTOM.

LAP JOINT

SIDE

BACK

LAP JOINT

BOTTOM

FRONT

DRAWER FACE

THIS PIECE IS THE TRUE WIDTH OF THE CABINET OPENING MINUS ¹⁄₁₆" CLEARANCE ON ALL SIDES.

TWO ¼" x ¾" WOOD CLEATS (STOCK ITEM BOUGHT AT LUMBER YARD)

Fig. 1-21

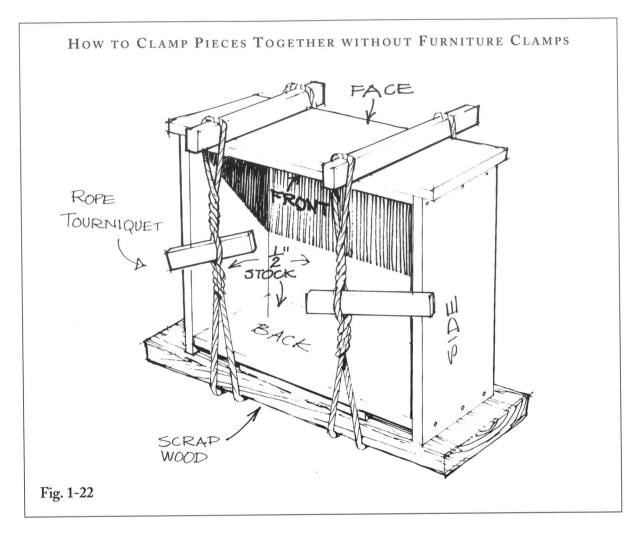

HOW TO CLAMP PIECES TOGETHER WITHOUT FURNITURE CLAMPS

FACE

ROPE
TOURNIQUET

FRONT

1"
2"
STOCK

BACK

SIDE

SCRAP
WOOD

Fig. 1-22

the drawer slightly smaller in width (at least ¹⁄₁₆ inch) than the opening.

2. The back and the front are identical in size. To make them, subtract 1 inch from the width of the drawer face and ¾ inch from the height of the true front (the drawer face). The sides are the same height as the face; their length is found by measuring the depth of the cabinet opening and subtracting ½ inch.

3. The bottom is the same width as the front and back. Its length is the same dimension as the sides minus ¼ inch.

4. The sides, front and back are glued and nailed (with 1½-inch finishing nails) to the bottom (see Fig. 1-22). Check several times to make absolutely sure that the drawer is square in all directions. One way to do this is to take the diago-

nal measurement between two corners and compare it with the measurement between the other two corners. They should be exactly the same. Note that before the glue has dried, it is important to place the drawer in the cabinet space to make sure it fits. If it doesn't, you can still pull it apart and make adjustments.

5. Glue and nail the ¼-inch by ¾-inch side cleats onto the sides of the drawer using ⅝-inch brads. Make sure the top cleats are level with the top of the drawer sides (see Fig. 1-21).

6. When the glue has dried, carefully mark where the ¼-inch by ¾-inch cleats should go on the inside of the cabinet walls. They should be ¾ inch below the top of the drawer. Temporarily nail them in place using ⅝-inch brads (do not glue yet!) and test the drawer to see if it slides

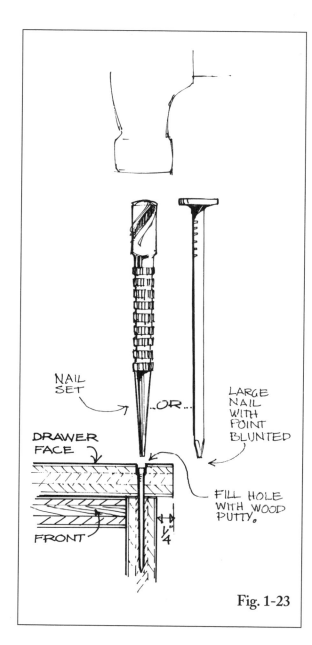

NAIL SET

...OR...

LARGE NAIL WITH POINT BLUNTED

DRAWER FACE

FILL HOLE WITH WOOD PUTTY.

FRONT

¼"

Fig. 1-23

Professional Flush Drawer

This type of drawer lasts longer than the simple lap joint but requires an electric router or table saw. These directions are also for a small or medium-sized drawer.

1. Cut all pieces from ½-inch stock except for the front, which is cut from ¾-inch stock, and the bottom, which is ¼-inch masonite. There is no "face" on this type of drawer. The front, back and sides are the same height as the cabinet opening, minus ⅛ inch for clearance. Be sure to label all the pieces so you know which side to cut.

2. The two side pieces are the full depth of the cabinet opening minus ¼ inch.

3. The back piece is the width of the cabinet opening minus ⅛ inch (allowing ¹⁄₁₆ inch on each side of the drawer for clearance) and minus an additional ¼ inch on each side (half the thickness of each drawer side), assuming you are using ½-inch stock.

4. The front is cut from ¾-inch stock, the same width as the cabinet face minus ⅛ inch for clearance.

5. Using an electric router or table saw, cut a ¼-inch-wide dado that is ¼ inch deep and ¼ inch from the bottom edge of all the pieces. This is the groove into which the bottom panel will fit.

6. Cut a dado ¹³⁄₁₆ inch wide and ¼ inch deep along the outside of both sides; it should start ¾ inch below the top edge.

7. From a piece of ¼-inch masonite, cut the bottom panel the same width as the back. Then cut the bottom panel so it is long enough to fit into the ¼-inch grooves in the back and front; it will be ½ inch longer than the interior of the drawer.

8. On the inside of the side pieces, make a vertical ¼-inch-deep dado that is ¼ inch wide (see Fig. 1-24) and ¼ inch from their back end to accept the back.

smoothly. Chances are it won't and the cleat will have to be removed and repositioned. If the nails start to go in the original holes again, take them out and start them in new spots.

7. When everything is nice and square and fits just right, nail and glue the drawer face to the completed drawer (see Fig. 1-22). Use thin 2-inch-long finishing nails and countersink them below the surface of the wood with a large blunt nail or a nail set (see Fig. 1-23).

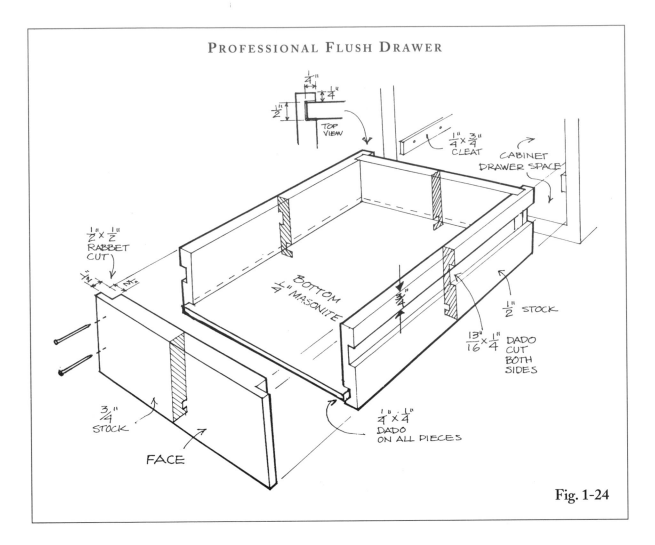

PROFESSIONAL FLUSH DRAWER

Fig. 1-24

9. On the back side of the front piece, make a ½-inch-wide rabbet that is ½ inch deep that will accept the sides.

10. Assemble the drawer without glue or nails and place it in the cabinet space to see if all the pieces fit together correctly. Then glue and nail the pieces together and place the drawer in the cabinet again for a final check before the glue hardens.

11. To make the drawer cleats, cut two strips that are ¼ inch by ¾ inch, making them ¼ inch shorter than the overall length of the space the drawer fits.

Nail them onto each side of the cabinet walls, placing them ¾ inch down from where the top of the drawer will be. Make sure they are parallel and even. Test to see if the drawer slides smoothly. If it doesn't fit perfectly, adjust the side cleats before finally gluing and nailing them permanently in place.

DRAWER SLIDES

Many professional carpenters insist that metal telescoping ball-bearing slides are the only way to hang a drawer. Indeed, they do pull smoothly and can be adjusted easily, but they also are expensive.

If you plan to use metal slides, you should generally leave ½-inch clearance on either side of the drawer (see Fig. 1-25). Follow the mounting directions on the package and screw the corresponding sections onto the sides of the drawer and the interior of the cabinet, driving the screws

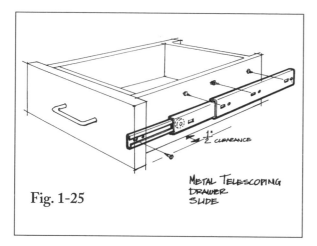

Fig. 1-25

METAL TELESCOPING
DRAWER
SLIDE

½" CLEARANCE

through the slotted holes. When you are sure the drawer fits properly, place screws in the round holes and drive them permanently in place.

SHELVES

One of the most necessary items in any child's room, regardless of age, is additional shelf space. People tend to build shelves more than anything else, probably because shelves appear so simple to construct. They are easy to build as long as you follow a few basic rules.

1. Draw plans to scale on paper and double-check your measurements.

2. If you use ¾-inch stock (such as 1x12s), don't make shelves span more than 3 feet without a support or they will bend in the middle under a heavy load. Note that ⁵⁄₄-inch stock is thicker, stronger and better looking than ¾-inch stock and can support up to 4-foot spans.

3. If you plan to have shelves against a wall, be aware of the baseboard at floor level and notch out the wood to allow for the molding.

4. Floors are rarely perfectly flat, so check them with a level and trim off the bottom of the shelves where necessary.

5. If the shelves are going to be higher than 3 feet, attach them to the wall so they cannot be pulled over accidentally.

6. If you are renting an apartment and plan to move in the near future, choose a design that you can disassemble and take with you when you leave.

7. The kind of wood to buy depends on a number of factors. If you plan on painting the shelves when you are finished, #2 common 1x12s are acceptable. To save time, give all the lumber a primer coat using a roller before assembling. The knots in #2 common lumber can bleed through paint, so be sure to use a good shellac-based sealer.

The best wood to buy for shelving is ⁵⁄₄-inch clear white pine stock, although it is expensive. Two alternatives are common 2x8s or 2x10s, if you like a rustic look. This lumber is actually 1½ inches thick and can take heavy loads. It can look quite attractive if stained a dark brown or ebony but requires too much sanding to make it suitable for painting, so don't consider using it if the room's decor is light and contemporary.

The simplest (but not the cheapest) shelves are 1x10s supported on metal brackets that are in turn attached to metal vertical standards (see Fig. 1-26). These are screwed to the studs in the wall with 1½-inch-long flathead screws. Be sure to

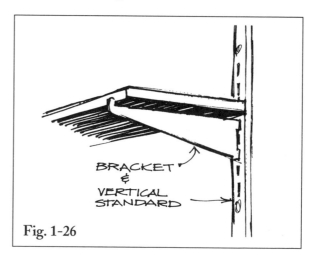

BRACKET
&
VERTICAL
STANDARD

Fig. 1-26

level the standards to the same height on the wall. The only problem with this system is that there is nothing at the ends of the shelf to keep objects from falling off.

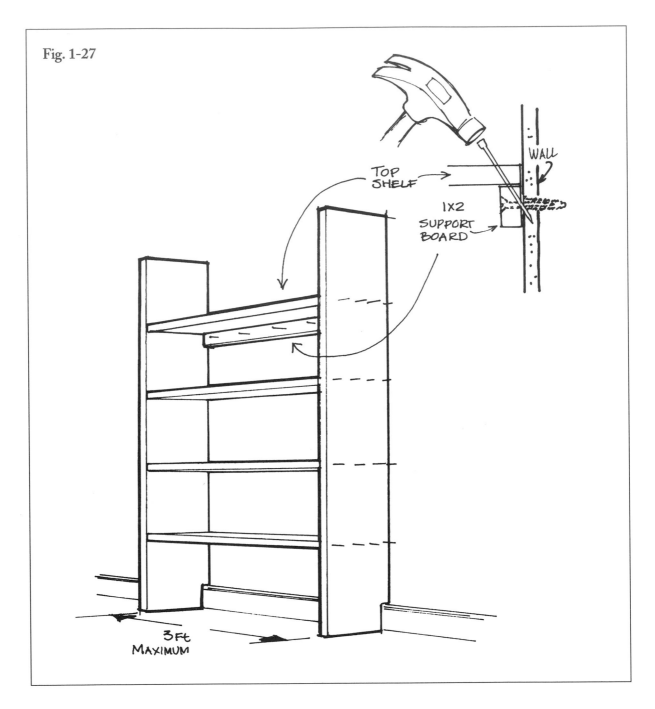

Fig. 1-27

TOP SHELF

WALL

1X2 SUPPORT BOARD

3 Ft MAXIMUM

The second simplest — and the cheapest — method of construction is the open standing shelf (see Fig. 1-27), which gives the objects to be stored a more enclosed look. The pieces can be precut at your lumberyard for an additional charge, so all you would then need to do is sand and nail them together. You can vary the number of shelves to suit your needs, but if you make high shelves, be sure to attach them to the wall.

This will also keep the shelves from moving out of square (racking).

HOW TO MAKE OPEN SHELVES

1. Measure the space you want the shelves to fit. Check the floor to make sure it's level and at right angles to the wall.

2. Draw a plan on a piece of paper indicating the height of the shelves. The depth is determined by the dimension of the boards you use.

Make sure when selecting the wide boards (1x10s and 1x12s) to avoid cupped or warped lumber.

3. You also can have shelves cut out of a 4x8 sheet of ¾-inch plywood, which will make them slightly stronger. However, the edges will need to be covered with wooden strips to give the shelving a more finished look. This can be done in two ways:

Nail a ¾-inch by ¼-inch clear pine wood strip onto the front edge of the shelf using finishing nails; set the nails and fill with wood putty (see Figs. 1-28 and 1-23). Alternatively, you can cover the edge with wood veneer tape (Fig. 1-29).

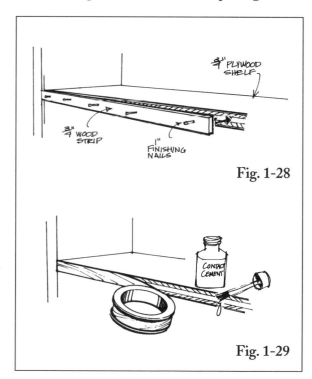

Fig. 1-28

Fig. 1-29

4. You may want to have the wood precut at the lumberyard. If you are using plywood, make sure to give the cutter a cutting plan. Remember, you pay for the whole piece of plywood, so make sure you get the scrap pieces with your order; they often can come in handy for other projects.

One advantage of using plywood is that you have a choice of surfaces to choose from. The most popular plywood is birch veneer. You can get birch tape that matches the face of the plywood to cover the rough edges.

5. If the wood is not precut, cut it to the desired lengths and lay the pieces on the floor in your child's room. If necessary, sand the wood and prime it while it is still unassembled. Fill any holes or knots with plastic wood or water-based wood putty and sand smooth.

6. Lay the two upright sides down on the floor next to each other with the outside edges facing down. Using a T-square, mark two lines where the shelves will go, marking across both boards at the same time (see Fig. 1-30).

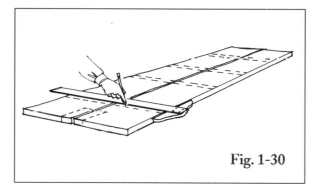

Fig. 1-30

7. Notch out the back lower edge to accept the baseboard (see Fig. 1-31) and, if necessary, trim off the bottom to conform to the irregularities of the floor.

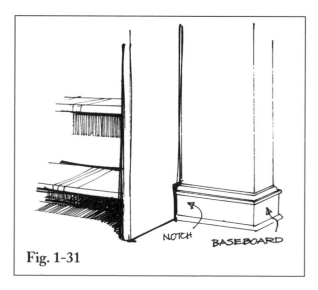

Fig. 1-31

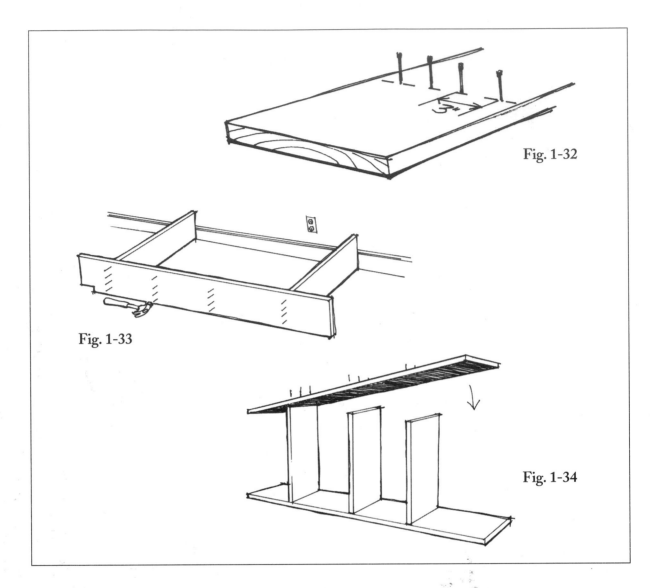

Fig. 1-32

Fig. 1-33

Fig. 1-34

8. Turn the two side boards over and mark with a light dashed line where the center of the shelf boards should go (see Fig. 1-32). Nail 3-inch finishing nails at 3-inch intervals across the marked board so their points are just protruding through the other side.

9. When you have started all the nails, turn a board up on its long edge. Position it at right angles to the wall and wedge two of the shelves between the wall and the side board to support it while nailing (see Fig. 1-33).

10. Make sure the shelves are in their proper position between the pencil lines you drew (see step 6 above) and hammer the nails. Repeat with the other shelves until all are completed.

11. Turn the structure over so that the shelves are pointing up and carefully position the second side over the ends of the shelves. Hammer the nails completely through, checking alignment as you go (see Fig. 1-34).

12. Stand the structure up, moving it into position so it is resting against the wall. Don't be upset by how weak it feels, as this will be corrected in the final step.

13. Carefully measure and cut a 1x2 support board and secure it to the wall directly under the top shelf (see Fig. 1-27). If possible, locate the wall studs (see instructions below on how to do this), screwing through the support board and wall and into the studs. You can also attach the

CHILD'S ART DESK, PAGE 101

KITCHEN CENTER, PAGE 109

COMPUTER CENTER, PAGE 120

PORTABLE STORAGE WAGON, PAGE 130

support board to the wall using wall anchors sold for this purpose. Then nail one 3-inch finishing nail every foot along the top shelf at an angle so that the nails penetrate the support board. This will make the shelf semipermanently attached to the wall and safer for your child (see Fig. 1-27).

HOW TO LOCATE WALL STUDS

Since most (but not all) houses built after World War II have studs spaced at 16-inch intervals on center, measure from the nearest corner in 16-inch increments and mark where you think the studs should be. Pound the wall with your fist and listen for the solidest sound.

To prevent the possibility of accidental shock, turn off the electricity in that section of the house at the fuse box or circuit breaker. Next, drive a long nail into the wall where you think the stud should be. If it hits something solid and is difficult to remove, you've probably found the stud. If not, open up the hole a little and probe with a screwdriver or coat hanger to the left and right to see if you can feel the stud. Mark where you think the stud is and make another exploratory hole.

When you're sure you are dead center over the stud, measure over 16 inches (sometimes 20 inches in older houses) and hammer in another nail. If you don't find a stud there, begin the same process over at the new location. If you are apprehensive about punching holes in your nice smooth wall, be assured that they can be easily patched with plaster spackle.

Spackle is sold wet or dry, and both are good for all kinds of jobs. To use dry spackle, mix it with water to a putty- or doughlike consistency. Using a 4-inch-wide flexible putty knife, a kitchen sandwich spreader or a spatula, fill the hole with spackle. After it has set for a few minutes, wipe it lightly with a flat wet sponge. Wait until after the spot has thoroughly dried before sanding it with fine sandpaper wrapped around a block of wood. Repeat the process if there are any remaining depressions. Finally, use the same paint color as the rest of the wall to touch up the spackle spots.

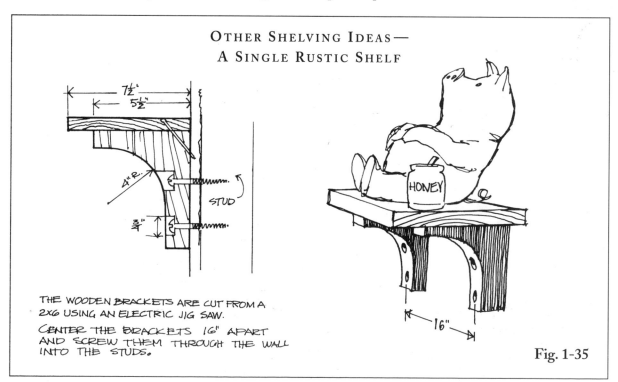

OTHER SHELVING IDEAS —
A SINGLE RUSTIC SHELF

7½"
5½"
4" R.
STUD
¾"

THE WOODEN BRACKETS ARE CUT FROM A 2×6 USING AN ELECTRIC JIG SAW.
CENTER THE BRACKETS 16" APART AND SCREW THEM THROUGH THE WALL INTO THE STUDS.

HONEY

16"

Fig. 1-35

METAL SHELF BRACKETS

Fig. 1-36

METAL BRACKETS ARE AVAILABLE AT HARDWARE STORES IN MANY SIZES.

IF THE SHELF IS INTENDED TO SUPPORT HEAVY OBJECTS, YOU MUST USE LEAD OR PLASTIC ANCHORS IN PLASTER WALLS.
NOTE: IT IS IMPORTANT TO DRILL THE CORRECT SIZE HOLE FOR THESE ANCHORS.— ASK YOUR HARDWARE SALESMAN FOR THE RIGHT DRILL.

COMBINATION SHELF AND CLOTHES RACK

Fig. 1-37

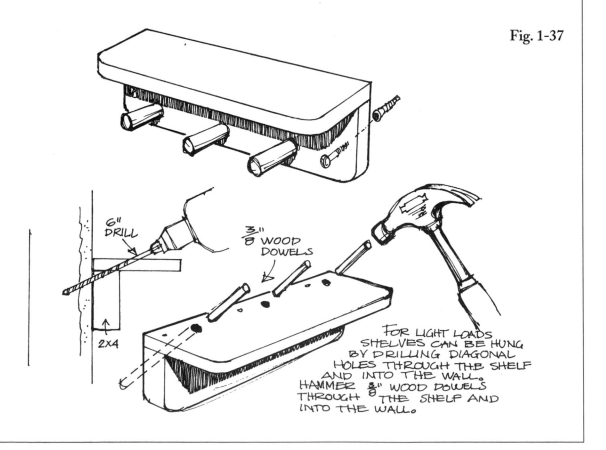

6" DRILL

3/8" WOOD DOWELS

2x4

FOR LIGHT LOADS SHELVES CAN BE HUNG BY DRILLING DIAGONAL HOLES THROUGH THE SHELF AND INTO THE WALL. HAMMER 3/8" WOOD DOWELS THROUGH THE SHELF AND INTO THE WALL.

MISCELLANEOUS SHELF HINTS

Fig. 1-38

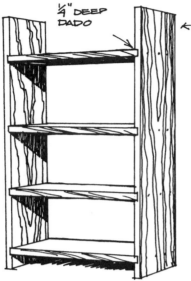

¼" DEEP DADO

← OPEN SHELVES MADE FROM 2"x 12" CONSTRUCTION LUMBER

TO INCREASE THE STRENGTH CUT DADOES IN THE VERTICAL SIDE SUPPORTS AND RECESS THE SHELVES IN ¼". BESIDES PROVIDING A REST FOR THE SHELF, THE DADO ALLOWS A GREATER GLUING AREA FOR THE JOINT.

CUT DADOES WITH A DOVETAIL SAW

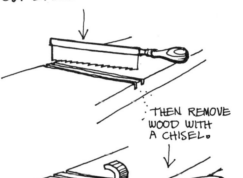

THEN REMOVE WOOD WITH A CHISEL.

STAIN THE SHELVES DARK TO HIDE THE IMPERFECTIONS OF THE ROUGH LUMBER.

OPEN SHELVES CAN BE MADE FREE-STANDING, SIMILAR TO A ROOM DIVIDER, BY SECURING THE UPRIGHT TO THE CEILING.

Fig. 1-39

TWO WAYS TO ATTACH THE UPRIGHTS TO THE CEILING

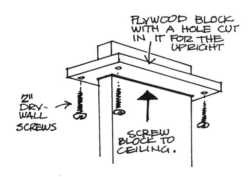

PLYWOOD BLOCK WITH A HOLE CUT IN IT FOR THE UPRIGHT

2" DRY-WALL SCREWS

SCREW BLOCK TO CEILING.

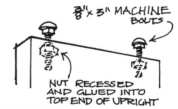

⅜" x 3" MACHINE BOLTS

NUT RECESSED AND GLUED INTO TOP END OF UPRIGHT

CUT UPRIGHTS 1" SHORTER THAN CEILING HEIGHT.
THREAD MACHINE BOLTS INTO RECESSED NUTS.
RAISE SHELVES AND UNSCREW BOLTS UNTIL THEY TOUCH CEILING.

Fig. 1-40

BUILDING PROJECTS

PROJECTS FOR BEGINNERS

SAWHORSES

TO BUILD MANY OF THE PROJECTS IN
this book, it is helpful to have a solid surface on which to lay your lumber while cutting.
These two sawhorses are a simple solution and take less than an hour to build. Made
from one 4x8 sheet of ¾-inch plywood, they fold up neatly and take little storage space
when not in use. And leftover plywood from this project can even be used to make the
Footstool (see page 50).

If you plan to store your sawhorses outdoors be sure to purchase exterior-grade or
pressure-treated plywood rather than birch veneer plywood, which is recommended for
most of the projects in this book.

<table>
<tr><td colspan="3" align="center">MATERIALS</td></tr>
<tr><td>**Quantity**</td><td>**Size**</td><td>**Description**</td></tr>
<tr><td>1</td><td>4x8 sheet</td><td>¾-inch exterior plywood</td></tr>
<tr><td>4 pairs</td><td>1 inch by 3½ inches</td><td>hinges with screws</td></tr>
</table>

Use a 48-inch-long T-square and a pencil to mark the sawhorse dimensions on the plywood (see Fig. 2-1). Next, rest the sheet of plywood on three 2x4s and check to make sure there is enough room for the electric jig saw blade to cut through the plywood without touching the floor. Clamp an 8-foot piece of a scrap 1x4 to the plywood to act as a straightedge while cutting (see page 21, Fig. 1-8).

Before cutting out the four 17-inch by 25-inch middle pieces, drill a starting hole inside the area you will be cutting out, using an electric drill with a ¼-inch spade bit. Place the saw blade in the hole before turning on the motor. Keep the saw pressed against the straightedge while cutting and always turn off the saw before removing the blade.

Cut out the four marked middle sections. Two of these pieces become the cross panels of the two sawhorses. The other two pieces can be saved for another project.

Drill another starting hole and cut out the 9-inch by 1½-inch slot (as shown in the cutting plan, Fig. 2-2). Because of the small dimensions, you will have to cut square corners when cutting the slots.

Remember that when using an electric jig saw, it is easier to cut rounded corners than square corners. When cutting out a square corner, however, take several small "bites" out of the waste side of the corner until there is enough room to turn the saw 90 degrees without the saw blade binding in the wood. Turn off the saw and reposition it before you begin the next cut.

Adjoin the legs of one set of sawhorses by attaching one pair of 3½-inch hinges to the tops of the sawhorse legs with a screwdriver (see Fig. 2-2). When screwing the hinges onto the plywood, make sure that the pin of each hinge is centered between the two pieces of plywood.

With another pair of hinges, attach the cross panel to the sawhorse leg as shown in the cutting plan. Stand up the sawhorse and pull down the cross panel so that the tab on the opposite leg fits into the slot in the cross panel. This completes the triangle and makes a strong support. If the tab does not fit perfectly into the slot, file off any excess material with a rasp. The tab should fit tightly. Repeat these steps for the second sawhorse.

Fig. 2-1

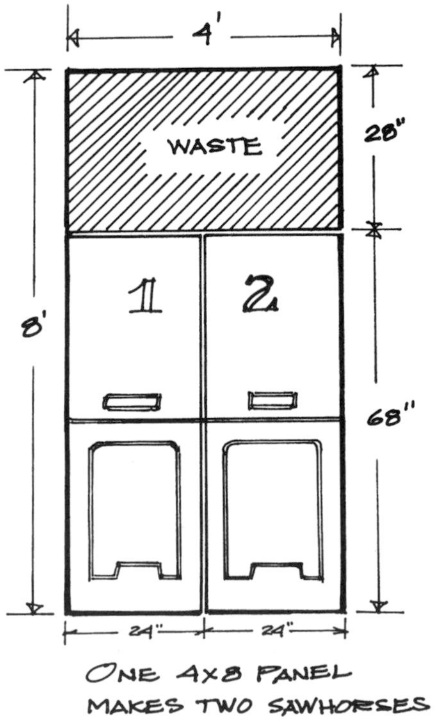

ONE 4X8 PANEL
MAKES TWO SAWHORSES

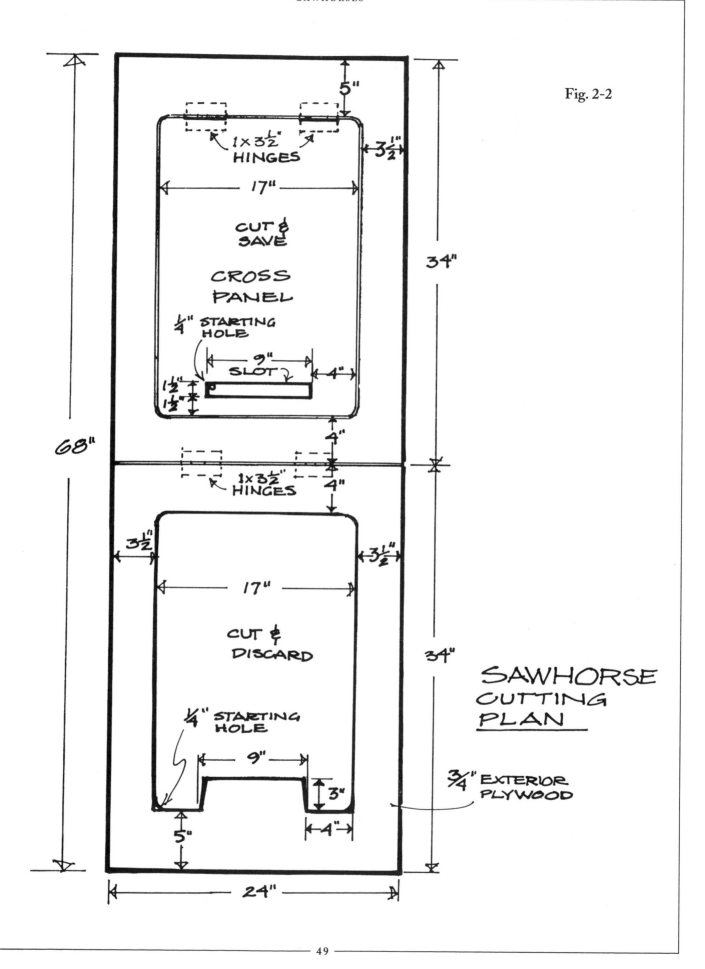

Fig. 2-2

5"

1 x 3½" HINGES

3½"

17"

CUT & SAVE

CROSS PANEL

34"

¼" STARTING HOLE

9"

SLOT

4"

1½"
1½"

68"

4"

1 x 3½" HINGES

4"

3½"

17"

3½"

CUT & DISCARD

34"

¼" STARTING HOLE

SAWHORSE CUTTING PLAN

9"

3"

3/4" EXTERIOR PLYWOOD

5"

4"

24"

FOOTSTOOL

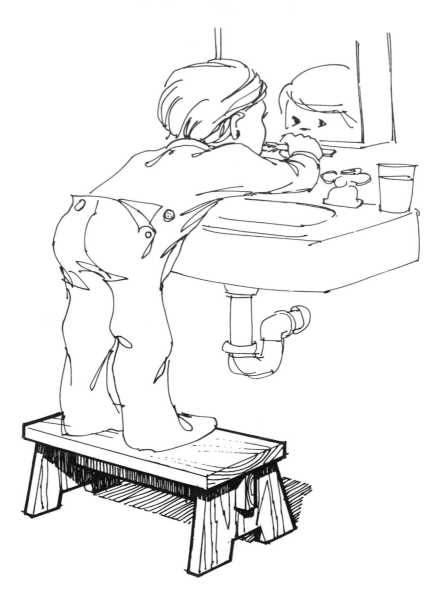

YOU CAN BUILD THIS SIMPLE FOOTSTOOL in less than an hour. It's an easy project to do with your kids and an excellent way to teach them many basic carpentry skills such as cutting, nailing, sanding and finishing.

Cut the pieces out of a 1x8 or from ¾-inch-thick plywood (or the scrap plywood left over from building the two sawhorses). The footstool can be used for many things — for kids brushing their teeth or adults putting the star on the top of the Christmas tree.

MATERIALS

Quantity	Size	Description	Location
1	4 feet	1x8 #2 or clear pine	legs, top, cross support
		or	
1	16 inches by 16¼ inches	¾-inch plywood	legs, top, cross support
1 box	2 inch	finishing nails	
1 pint		polyurethane	
		or enamel paint	

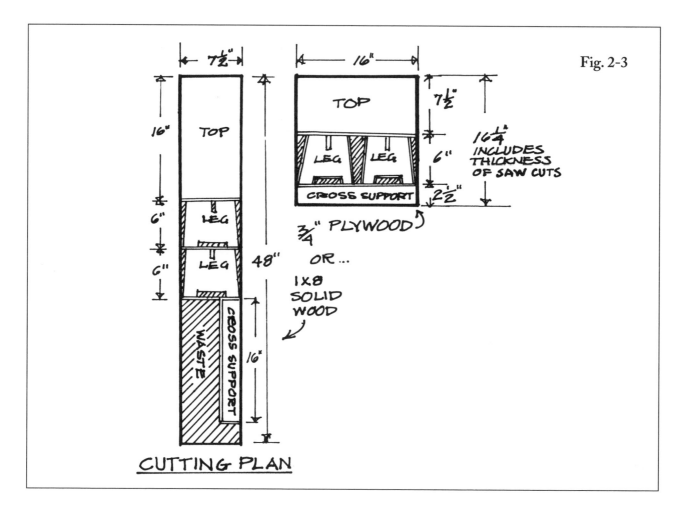

Fig. 2-3

CUTTING PLAN

Referring to the cutting plan (see Fig. 2-3), cut out the pieces with an electric jig saw. Cut a ¾-inch by 2½-inch slot in the top center of each leg piece (see Fig. 2-4).

Since the thickness of lumber can vary slightly, make sure to cut the two leg slots exactly the same dimension as the thickness of the wood you are using to ensure that the cross support will fit snugly into the slots.

Next, decide which side of the wood is of better quality and make sure that this side is the one that will show. Apply glue inside the two leg slots and

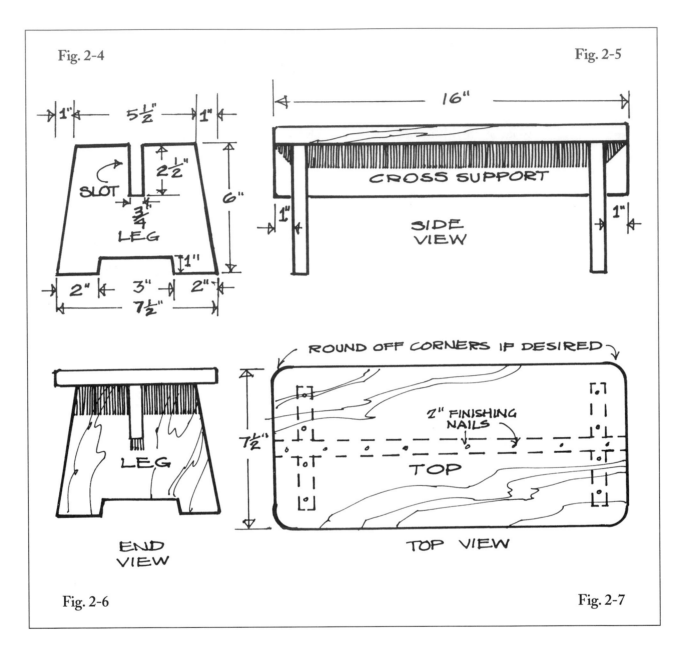

Fig. 2-4

Fig. 2-5

SLOT
LEG

SIDE VIEW

CROSS SUPPORT

END VIEW
LEG

TOP VIEW

ROUND OFF CORNERS IF DESIRED

2" FINISHING NAILS

TOP

Fig. 2-6

Fig. 2-7

slide the cross piece down into them, allowing for a 1-inch overhang on each side of the legs.

Remember before gluing the pieces together to lay the better side of the top piece face down on the floor or workbench and to mark with a pencil where the legs and cross support will be attached. Then position and glue the cross support and legs to the underside of the stool top (see Figs. 2-5 and 2-6). Reinforce the footstool with 2-inch finishing nails every 2 inches (see Fig. 2-7). Sand and finish the footstool with polyurethane or a bright enamel paint.

PORTABLE FOLDING TABLE

THIS PORTABLE TABLE IS IDEAL FOR A teenager who is going off to boarding school or college, where there never seems to be enough storage or flat surface space. Our daughter was happy to be able to have this table for her room at college, for it folds up neatly for transporting or storing. The leg supports can be easily removed, folded flat and stored underneath the table in the recess created by the 1-inch by 2-inch lip.

We recommend using melamine particleboard and trimming the edges with a clear pine 1x2. Finish the table by applying three coats of polyurethane to the wood and sealing the exposed edges with melamine banding.

<table>
<tr><td colspan="4" align="center">MATERIALS</td></tr>
<tr><td>Quantity</td><td>Size</td><td>Description</td><td>Location</td></tr>
<tr><td>1</td><td>4x4 sheet</td><td>¾-inch melamine particleboard</td><td>table top, leg supports</td></tr>
<tr><td>1</td><td>12 feet</td><td>1x2 clear pine</td><td>table-top edging</td></tr>
<tr><td>2</td><td>12 inches</td><td>¾-inch by ¾-inch piano hinges
with screws</td><td>leg supports</td></tr>
<tr><td>8</td><td>¾ inch long</td><td>¼-inch dia. wooden pegs</td><td>leg supports</td></tr>
<tr><td>8</td><td>⅝ inch long</td><td>¾-inch dia. nylon glide tacks</td><td></td></tr>
<tr><td>1</td><td>¾-inch roll</td><td>melamine banding</td><td></td></tr>
<tr><td>1 pint</td><td></td><td>polyurethane</td><td></td></tr>
<tr><td>1 box</td><td>2 inch</td><td>finishing nails</td><td></td></tr>
</table>

Referring to the cutting plan (see Fig. 2-9), cut out all the pieces using a portable electric circular or table saw with a carbide-tooth blade. Attach two of the 12-inch pieces with one of the piano hinges and do the same with the other two 12-inch pieces, forming the two leg supports. After screwing the hinges to the leg supports, finish off the exposed edges by covering them with iron-on melamine banding.

To make the pine edging for the table top, use a miter box (see miter box, page 12) or a table saw to cut two 49½-inch-long pieces of 1x2 clear pine at a 45-degree angle; the edging should meet perfectly at the corners (see detail in Fig. 2-8). Glue and nail the pine edging to the table-top edges using 2-inch finishing nails. Sink the nail heads, fill the holes with wood putty and sand smooth (see detail in Fig. 1-23, page 31). Paint the pine edging with three coats of polyurethane, sanding lightly between each coat.

To protect the floor and to allow the table to slide more easily, hammer a ¾-inch diameter nylon glide tack to the bottom of each leg support; there will be a total of eight nylon tacks. Attach the leg supports to the underside of the table top by drilling ¼-inch-wide by ⅜-inch-deep holes in the top of the supports, approximately 1 inch from each end. Cut four ¼-inch diameter pegs that are ¾ inch long and glue and tap the pegs into the holes so that ⅜ inch of each peg protrudes from the top of the hole. Round off the tops of each peg with a file. Position the leg supports so they fit into the inside corners of the table. Mark where the pegs touch the underneath side of the table top and carefully bore a ¼-inch by ⅜-inch hole at the marks. Be careful not to drill too deeply or the bit will go through the top of the table! Position the table top over the pegs on the supports and pound on the table top with the palm of your hand until it fits into place.

When moving the table, do not lift it by the top or the leg supports will be pulled off. (They are meant to be easily removed and stored in the recess under the table top.) Instead, always slide the table to its new position.

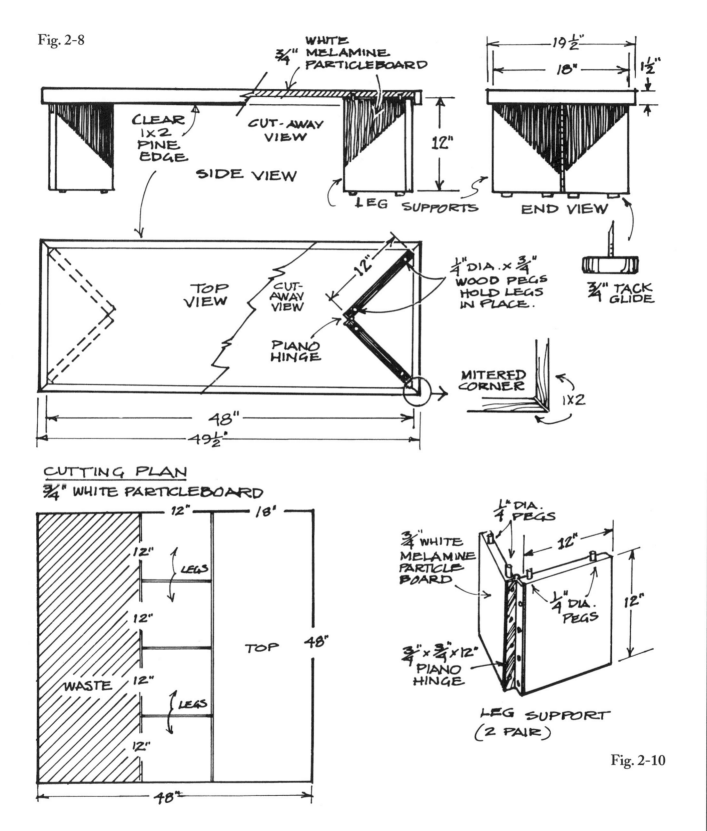

Fig. 2-8

WHITE MELAMINE PARTICLEBOARD
3/4"

CLEAR 1x2 PINE EDGE

CUT-AWAY VIEW

SIDE VIEW

LEG SUPPORTS

19 1/2"
18"
1 1/2"

12"

END VIEW

3/4" TACK GLIDE

TOP VIEW

CUT-AWAY VIEW

12"

1/4" DIA. x 3/4" WOOD PEGS HOLD LEGS IN PLACE.

PIANO HINGE

MITERED CORNER
1x2

48"
49 1/2"

CUTTING PLAN
3/4" WHITE PARTICLEBOARD

WASTE

12"
12"   LEGS
12"
12"   LEGS
12"

18"
TOP   48"

48"

Fig. 2-9

1/4" DIA. PEGS

3/4" WHITE MELAMINE PARTICLE BOARD

12"

1/4" DIA. PEGS

12"

3/4" x 3/4" x 12" PIANO HINGE

LEG SUPPORT (2 PAIR)

Fig. 2-10

ROOM DIVIDER

A ROOM DIVIDER IS AN INEXPENSIVE and easy project to construct. It can be used as a screen to conceal toy bins, hampers or tricycles or to give a sense of privacy to kids who are sharing a room. It also works well as a partition for a study or work area. If double-action hinges are used, the screens can be angled in any direction and can actually create two private spaces.

Homosote is the material of choice for the core of the divider. Soft, rigid but non-structural, it is often used for bulletin boards and other similar items. Cover the divider with any type of material (such as felt, colored burlap, fabric or wallpaper) and let your child decorate the panels with felt flowers, stars and moon faces or with colored fall leaves or snowmen that can be changed with the seasons. Artwork can be displayed and collages created right on the surface of the panels.

A decorative screen is an excellent and practical way to provide instant privacy or to make two spaces out of one. After your child outgrows it, you may want to re-cover the divider for yourself and partition off a dining area in a living room or kitchen or a dressing area in the master bedroom. Its uses are endless.

MATERIALS

Quantity	Size	Description	Location
1	4x8sheet	½-inch homosote	panels
8	10 feet	¼-inch by 1⅜-inch lattice	frame
4	10 feet	⅝-inch by ¼-inch pine molding	frame
3 pairs	¾ inch by 1¾ inch	double-action hinges and screws	
6	18 inches by 60 inches	decorative material	panel covering
6	1 inch	nylon glide tacks	feet
1 box	¾ inch	brads	
1 box	1¼ inch	finishing nails	
1 can		spray adhesive	panels
1 pint		polyurethane or enamel paint	lattice

OPTIONAL MATERIALS

2	1½ inch	½-inch dia. dowels	top corners
2		1½ inch dia. birch balls	top corners

I f you can't find birch balls at your local lumber-yard, you can order them from the Woodworkers' Store (see Sources).

Referring to the cutting plan (see Fig. 2-12), cut three 59½-inch by 16-inch panels from the homosote. To frame the panels, cut the twelve pieces of ¼-inch by 1⅜-inch lattice 60 inches long for the sides, and twelve pieces of ¼-inch by 1⅜-inch lattice 16½ inches long for the top and bottom pieces of the frame (see Fig. 2-13). Use a miter box to cut off the ends of the lattice strips at 45-degree angles so they will fit together squarely (see page 12 and Fig. 2-11).

For the side edges of the frame, miter-cut six pieces of ¼-inch by ⅝-inch pine molding, 60 inches long. For the top and bottom edges of the frame, cut six pieces 16½ inches long. This molding is sandwiched between the front and back lattice strips and strengthens the framing (see Figs. 2-14 and 2-15).

Measure and cut six pieces of felt, burlap or decorative fabric to cover the homosote on each side.

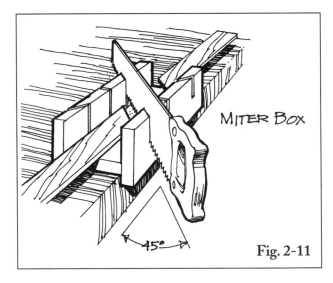

MITER BOX

45°

Fig. 2-11

Using spray adhesive, cover each piece of homosote and carefully lay the material over the homosote, smoothing out any wrinkles. Trim off any excess material that overlaps the sides. Glue and nail the ¼-inch by ⅝-inch molding with 1¼-inch finishing nails to the outside edges of the homosote.

When the glue has dried, frame the front and back of the panels by gluing and nailing the lattice strips around the perimeter of the panels using

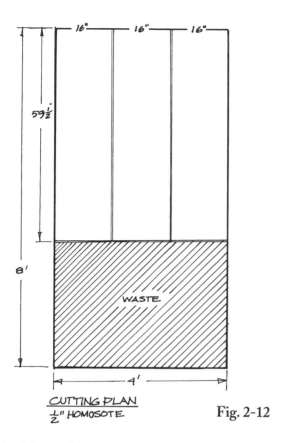

CUTTING PLAN
½" HOMOSOTE

16" 16" 16"

59½"

8'

WASTE

4'

Fig. 2-12

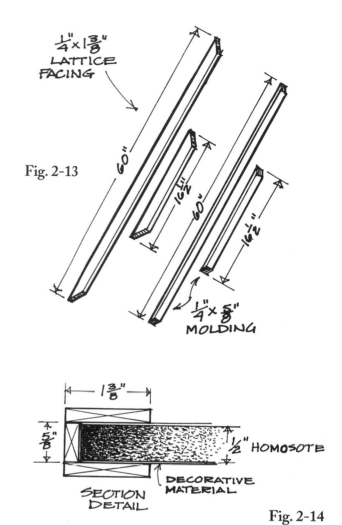

¼" x 1⅜" LATTICE FACING

60"

16½"

60"

16½"

¼" x ⅝" MOLDING

Fig. 2-13

1⅜"

⅝"

½" HOMOSOTE

DECORATIVE MATERIAL

SECTION DETAIL

Fig. 2-14

¾-inch brads. Make sure that the mitered corners fit neatly. The top of the frame should be flush with the top of the molding (see Fig. 2-15).

When the glue has dried, join the panels together by screwing three pairs of ¾-inch by 1¾-inch double-action hinges to the three panels. Standard hinges work fine but double-action hinges give you more flexibility.

If you wish, bore a ½-inch hole in the top of the outer corner of each of the two end panels and glue and insert a ½-inch diameter by 1½-inch-long dowel into each hole. Glue a 1½-inch-diameter birch ball onto each dowel. Nail two nylon glide tacks to the bottom of each panel to protect the floor from scratches.

Apply three coats of enamel paint or polyurethane to the frame. To protect the decorative screen while you are painting, slide a piece of scrap paper between the frame and the panel.

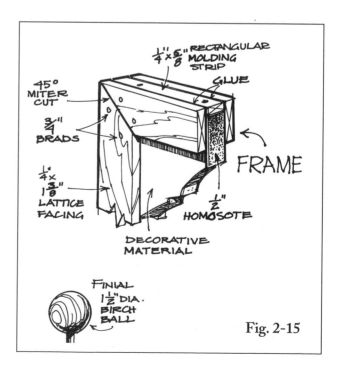

¼" x ⅝" RECTANGULAR MOLDING STRIP

GLUE

45° MITER CUT

¾" BRADS

¼ x 1⅜" LATTICE FACING

½" HOMOSOTE

FRAME

DECORATIVE MATERIAL

FINAL 1½" DIA. BIRCH BALL

Fig. 2-15

SLEEPING

CRIB

IF YOU'VE EVER TRIED TO ASSEMBLE
a standard child's crib, you'll appreciate the simplicity of this design. It can be assembled
and disassembled easily without complicated directions or tools. As with all cribs, it
should probably be assembled in the child's room since standard-width cribs are too wide
to fit through most door openings. This crib is essentially composed of two plywood side
panels, a flat support panel, a center divider for added strength, a shelf and four poles.

The front can be unlocked and swung down out of the way when changing the bed
sheets. The top rails are protected by two pieces of 1⅜-inch diameter clear vinyl tubing,
which can be bought through marine hardware suppliers (see Sources). Vinyl is extremely
safe and, since it's nontoxic, provides an excellent surface for a baby to teethe on.

This crib uses a standard 27¼-inch by 52-inch by 5½-inch mattress available at baby
supply stores. It has a shelf underneath on one side for diapers, blankets and toys and a
shelf on the other side to store seldom-needed items such as out-of-season clothes. A
soft nylon rope netting is used on two sides instead of the rigid bars found on most con-
ventional cribs. After the child outgrows the crib, it can be converted into a couch or seat.

MATERIALS

Quantity	Size	Description	Location
2	4x8 sheets	¾-inch plywood	ends, bedboard, shelf and center divider
4	54 inches	1⅜-inch dia. wood dowels	rails
2	1 inch	1⅜-inch dia. wood dowels	lock knobs
2	2 inches	⅜-inch dia. wood dowels	pegs for knobs
4	20 inches	¾-inch dia. wood dowels	side posts
2	53 inches	1 inch by ¼-inch clear pine	face strip
2	50 inches	1⅜-inch dia. clear vinyl tubing	railing
8	3½ inches	⁵⁄₁₆-inch dia. carriage bolts	
1 roll	2 feet by 20 feet	nylon safety netting	sides
1 roll	50 feet	nylon string	sides
1 quart		polyurethane or enamel paint	
4	3 inch dia.	casters (plate type)	bottom
16	½ inch	#8 roundhead screws	

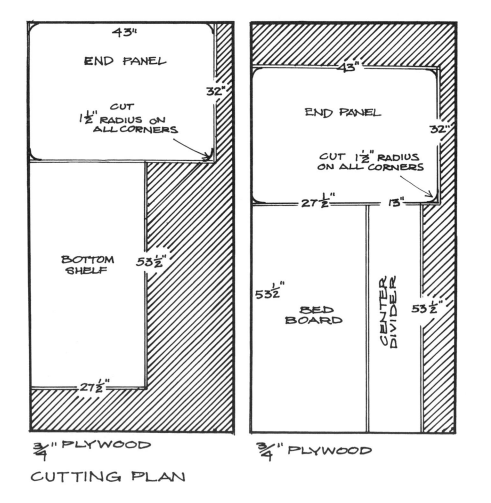

Fig. 2-16

CUTTING PLAN

eferring to the cutting plan (see Fig. 2-16), cut out the plywood pieces and round off the corners and edges (see page 26). Using a 1⅜-inch spade drill bit, cut 1⅜-inch diameter holes for the two bottom rails and one of the top rails. The other top rail hole will be smaller and is cut later (see Fig. 2-17 for hole locations).

In order for the crib to be strong, a total of eight dadoes are cut in the end panels, bed board and bottom shelf (see Figs. 2-17 and 2-24). Although using an electric router is the quickest method to make dadoes, they can also be made with a hammer and chisel (see Fig. 2-35, page 77). It will take about two hours per panel using a chisel. The bed board, center divider and bottom shelf are all cut 53½ inches long, and the edge of each piece fits into the ¼-inch dadoes on each end. Cut a ¾-inch-wide by ¼-inch-deep dado down the center of the bed board and the bottom shelf. The divider is cut 13 inches high, allowing ¼ inch to fit into the bed board

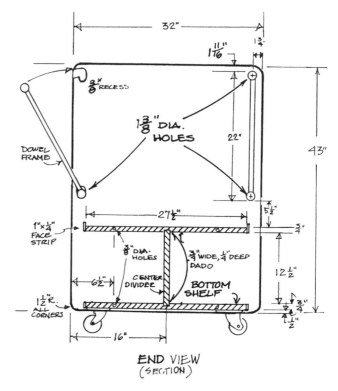

END VIEW
(SECTION)

Fig. 2-17

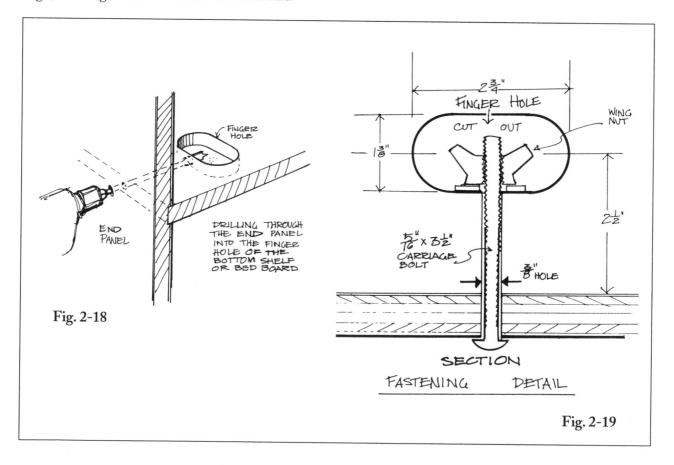

Fig. 2-18

SECTION
FASTENING DETAIL

Fig. 2-19

above and the bottom shelf below. Test the pieces to see that they fit easily into their prospective grooves.

As mentioned earlier, the crib can be assembled and disassembled easily because all the fastening is done with bolts and wing nuts. Holes are cut out around the wing nuts to allow space for fingers to turn them. These holes can be made with the same 1⅜-inch spade bit you use for the rail holes.

To make the bolt holes align properly, hold the bottom shelf or bed board and end panel pieces together and mark where the bolt holes should go. Remove the bed board or bottom shelf and, using a ⅜-inch spade bit, start the hole in the dado on the end panel. As you see the point begin to come through the other side, stop drilling and finish the hole from the outside of the end panel. Then position the two pieces together again. Drill through the hole in the end panel and into the edge of the ad-

joining plywood until you come all the way through into the finger hole (see Figs. 2-18 and 2-19).

Drill slowly and check frequently to see that the drill is straight. An oversized ⅜-inch hole is made in case of slight variations in the final alignment. Follow this same procedure for all twelve finger holes.

The lock knob is a safety catch and holds the top front rail in place. It's made by boring a ⅜-inch diameter hole in the center of a 1⅜-inch diameter knob and a similar hole through the side panel and into the center of the top rail (see Fig. 2-20). Glue a ⅜-inch diameter by 1½-inch-long peg into the knob.

Sand all edges smooth using wood putty where needed. Give all wood surfaces three coats of polyurethane.

Fig. 2-20   Fig. 2-21

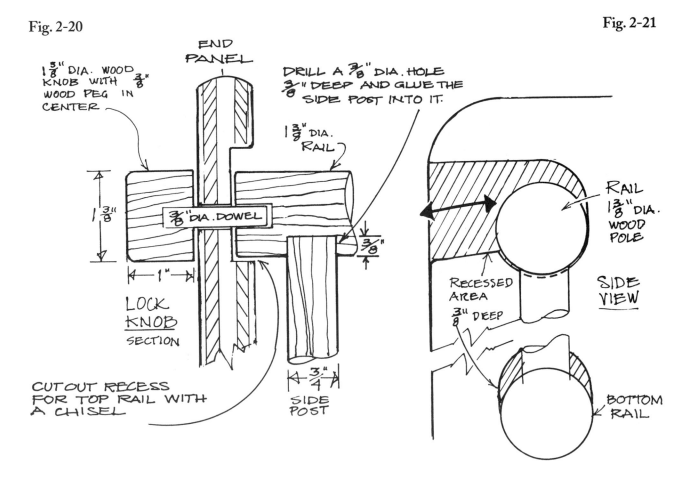

Fig. 2-22

TOP VIEW

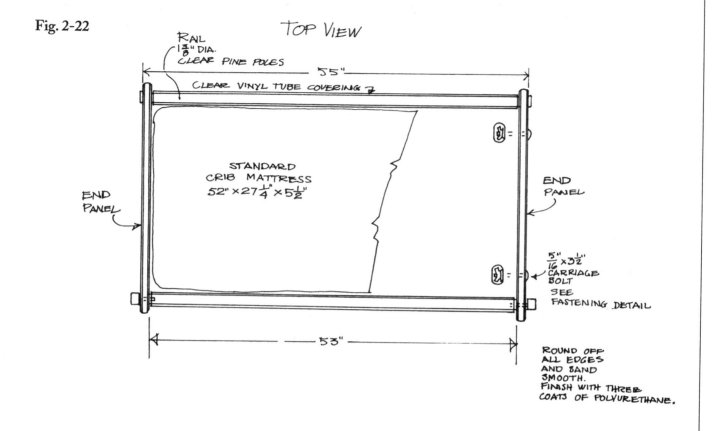

RAIL
1⅜" DIA.
CLEAR PINE POLES

CLEAR VINYL TUBE COVERING

55"

END PANEL

END PANEL

STANDARD
CRIB MATTRESS
52" × 27¼" × 5½"

5/16" × 3½"
CARRIAGE
BOLT
SEE
FASTENING DETAIL

53"

ROUND OFF
ALL EDGES
AND SAND
SMOOTH.
FINISH WITH THREE
COATS OF POLYURETHANE.

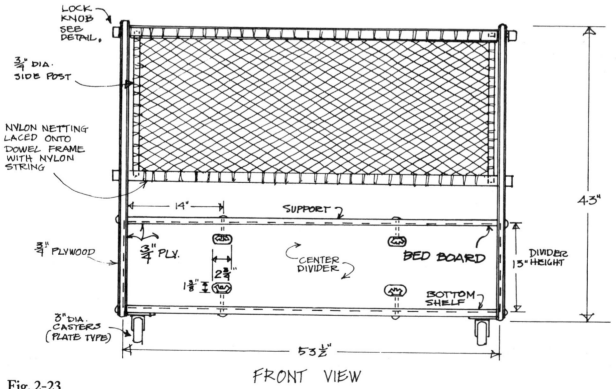

LOCK
KNOB
SEE
DETAIL.

¾" DIA.
SIDE POST

NYLON NETTING
LACED ONTO
DOWEL FRAME
WITH NYLON
STRING

43"

14"

SUPPORT

¾" PLYWOOD

¾" PLY.

2¾"

1⅜"

CENTER
DIVIDER

BED BOARD

DIVIDER
15" HEIGHT

3" DIA.
CASTERS
(PLATE TYPE)

BOTTOM
SHELF

53½"

FRONT VIEW

Fig. 2-23

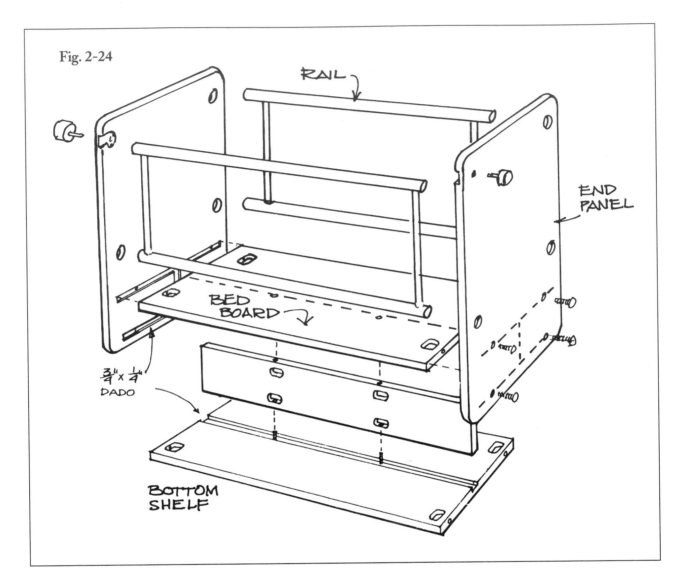

Fig. 2-24

RAIL

END PANEL

BED BOARD

3/4" x 1/4" DADO

BOTTOM SHELF

Attach the netting to the rails using white nylon string. Cut the protective vinyl tubing lengthwise with scissors and slip it over the two top rails (see Fig. 2-22). It stays in place of its own accord and can be removed if necessary.

Attach the casters to the underside of the bottom shelf (see Figs. 2-17 and 2-23), using #8 roundhead screws.

SAFETY TIPS: As a safety precaution, two distinct actions are necessary in order to unlock the front rail. After partially pulling the knobs out on both ends, the railing must be lifted up before it can be swung out and down.

The U.S. Consumer Product Safety Commission also recommends that the mattress fits snugly between the sides and rails. You should not be able to fit the width of more than two fingers between the mattress and the sides of the crib. For this reason, it's best to buy the mattress first and adjust the crib dimensions accordingly.

Also, avoid using old paint on a crib since the paint might contain lead and you may run the risk of lead poisoning.

THE CRIB BECOMES A COUCH

When your child outgrows the crib, it can be easily changed into a couch with storage underneath, and can even double as an extra bed for small friends who come to stay overnight (see Figs. 2-25 and 2-26).

Simply cut down the two end panels with an electric jig saw and add a back panel to give support to the two new bolsters. Round off all corners and edges and paint with polyurethane or enamel paint. Cover the crib mattress and bolsters in an attractive fabric.

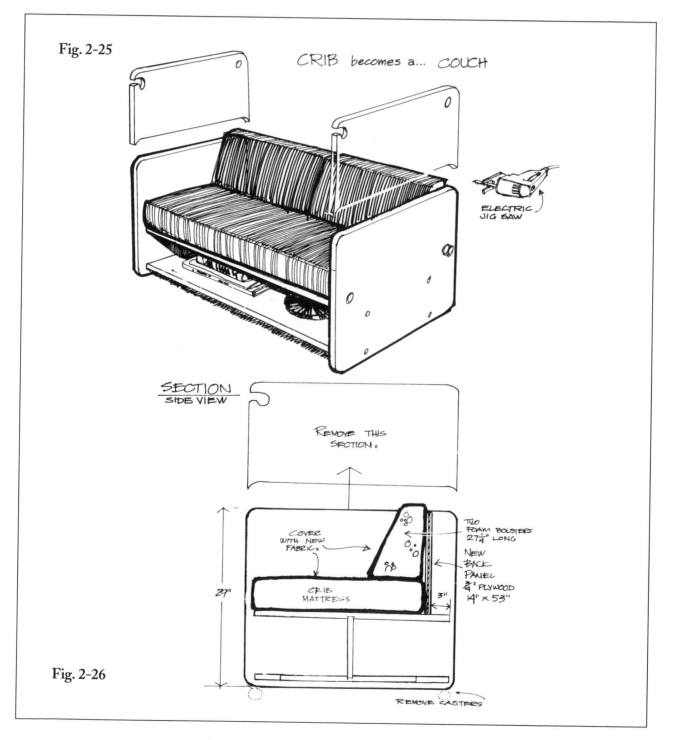

Fig. 2-25

CRIB becomes a... COUCH

ELECTRIC JIG SAW

SECTION
SIDE VIEW

REMOVE THIS SECTION.

COVER WITH NEW FABRIC.

CRIB MATTRESS

TWO FOAM BOLSTERS 27¼" LONG

NEW BACK PANEL ¾" PLYWOOD 14" x 53"

29"

3"

Fig. 2-26

REMOVE CASTERS

CHILD'S BED

WHEN YOUR CHILD HAS OUTGROWN A crib (generally around age four) you are faced with the problem of what size bed to invest in next. You could buy a youth bed; they typically measure 33 inches by 66 inches but will be quickly outgrown and locating the right sheets is often difficult. A wiser solution is to make the jump to a standard twin bed; they measure 39 inches by 75 inches. You'll also always be able to find sheets and blankets to fit it. Before you build the bed, however, buy the mattress and check the actual measurements to be sure they actually are 39 inches by 75 inches since mattress sizes often vary somewhat. You may need to adjust these dimensions slightly.

Until your child gets used to having no sides on the bed, you may want to place the bed next to a wall and put a pillow under the outside edge of the mattress to slope it slightly upward.

MATERIALS

Quantity	Size	Description	Location
1	4x8 sheet	¾-inch A/D plywood	bottom, ends, side board and support cleats
1	8 feet	1x8 #2 pine	side board
1	6 feet	4x4 #2 pine	post legs
1 box	1½ inch	finishing nails	
1 box	1½ inch	#10 flathead screws	
1 roll	¾ inch	wood veneer banding	
1 quart		polyurethane or enamel paint	

Fig. 2-27

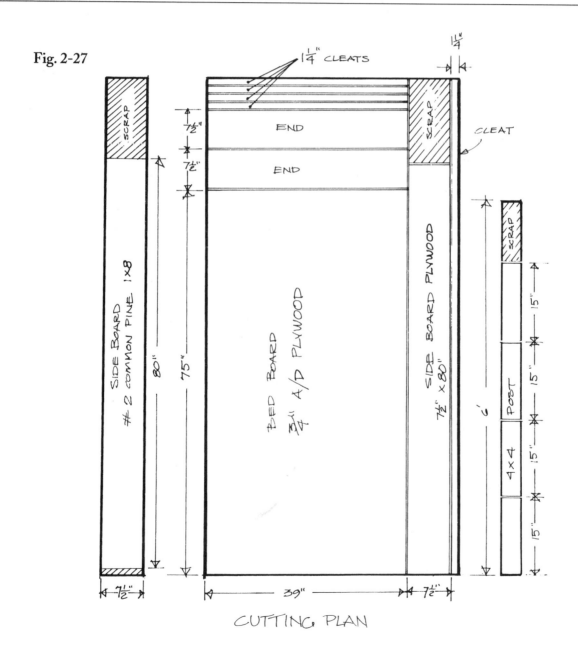

CUTTING PLAN

Fig. 2-28

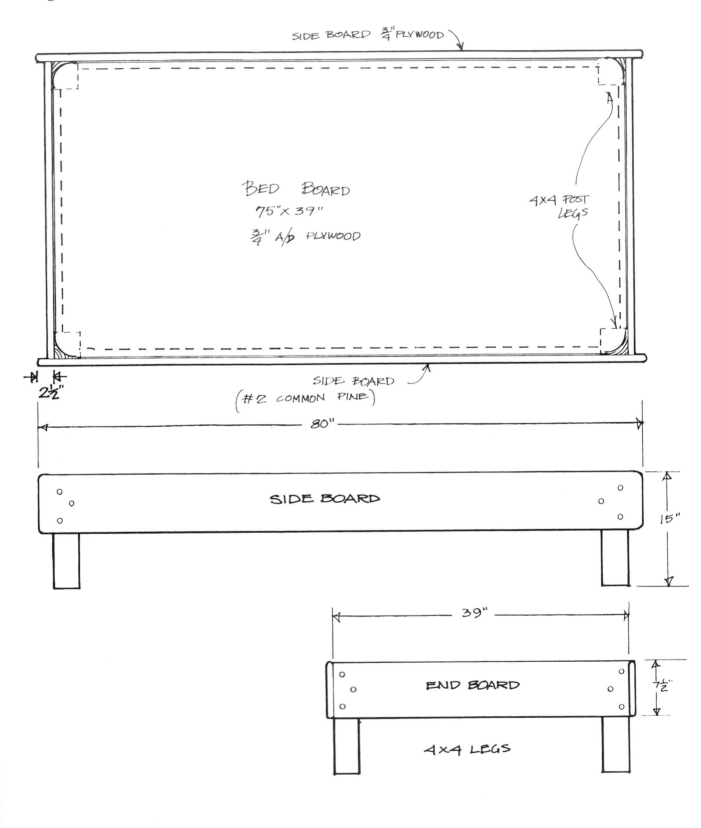

SIDE BOARD ¾" PLYWOOD

BED BOARD
75" X 39"
¾" A/D PLYWOOD

4X4 POST LEGS

SIDE BOARD
(#2 COMMON PINE)

2½"

80"

SIDE BOARD

15"

39"

END BOARD

7½"

4X4 LEGS

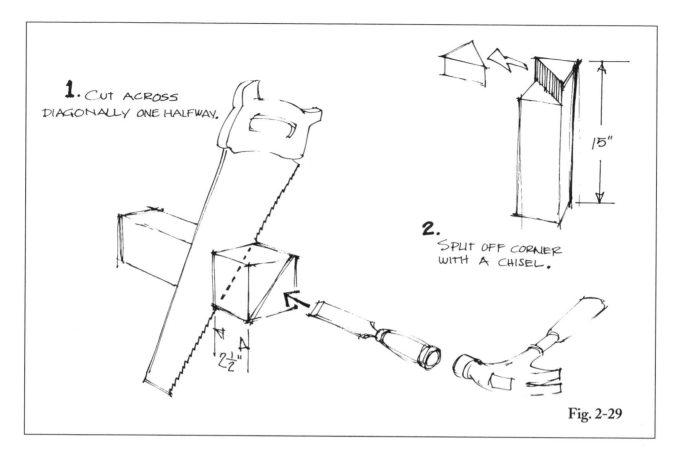

1. CUT ACROSS DIAGONALLY ONE HALFWAY.

2½"

15"

2. SPLIT OFF CORNER WITH A CHISEL.

Fig. 2-29

The child's bed is made from one sheet of ¾-inch plywood plus one 8-foot-long 1x8 for one of the side boards. (I designed this project to have a minimum amount of waste, which is why one side board is cut from a 1x8 — there isn't enough room on the 4x8 plywood sheet to fit both side boards. However, you may prefer that they both be the same.) Since the 1x8 side board is going to show, pick it out yourself from the stack of common lumber at your lumberyard, trying to find a piece that has as few knots as possible. Make sure the wood is straight — not warped — and clean. If necessary, take it out of the storage shed and examine it in daylight before accepting it.

It is also worthwhile to note that although you will need only a 5-foot length of a 4x4 post for the legs, the lumberyard will probably require you to buy a full 6- or 8-foot-long piece.

Before cutting out all the pieces to the specifica-

tions shown in the cutting plan (see Fig. 2-27), be sure to check the ends of the 1x8 since they may not be square and may even have marks on them. If either case is true, cut off 1 inch or so and then mark off 80 inches from this point on.

Make sure the two end boards are *exactly* the same length as the width of the bed board (39 inches). Cut off each corner of the bed board to accept the legs (see Fig. 2-32).

To make the legs, cut the 4x4 post into four 15-inch lengths. Cut a 2½-inch triangular piece out of the top of each post to allow space for the mattress corners (see Fig. 2-29). Place two of the 15-inch leg posts on the floor 75 inches apart and lay one of the side boards over them, making sure that the tops of the board and the legs are even. Screw the side board onto the two legs using #10 1½-inch flathead screws, but be sure to drill pilot holes for the screws first. Repeat the same step for the other side.

PROCEDURE FOR SCREWING THE SIDE AND END BOARDS TO THE LEGS

1. Mark the exact location for each screw.
2. Drill a ½-inch diameter hole ¼ inch deep.
3. Drill a hole the same size or slightly larger through the board.
4. Drill a hole slightly smaller into the leg (pilot hole).
5. Screw a #10 1½ inch flathead screw into the hole.
6. Fill the remaining ½-inch diameter hole with a wood dowel or wood filler.

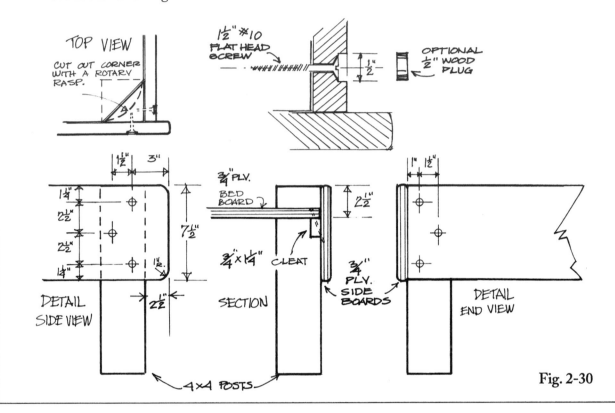

Fig. 2-30

Turn over the side boards and, using wood glue and nails, attach the 1¼-inches by ¾-inch support cleats to the side boards between the legs and 2½-inches down from the board tops. These supports must be cut to fit between the leg posts (see Fig. 2-31).

After rounding off the corners of the front side boards with a jig saw and sanding their edges round, prop up one of the side boards and place the edge of the bed board onto the cleat. Nail the bed board onto the cleat (see Fig. 2-32), leaving the nail heads protruding ½ inch in case you need to make an adjustment. Do the same for the other side. Attach the two end boards to the leg posts using #10 1½-inch screws (see Fig. 2-30). Cut and nail the remaining two support cleats to the end boards between the legs (see Fig. 2-31).

When the bed is completely assembled, check to see that all joints fit properly, make any necessary adjustments and then hammer the nails in all the way. If desired, fill the ½-inch diameter screw holes with a wooden plug or wood putty (see Fig. 2-30).

Set your mattress on the bed to see how it fits. If the corners are too tight, carve out an inside curve with a rotary rasp using an electric drill (see Fig. 2-33).

Fig. 2-31

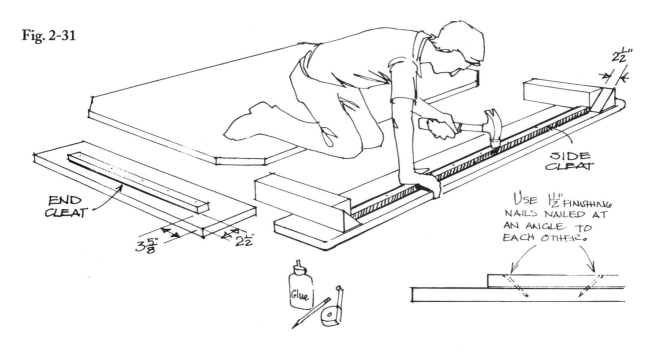

END CLEAT

3 5/8"

2 1/2"

2 1/2"

SIDE CLEAT

USE 1 1/2" FINISHING NAILS NAILED AT AN ANGLE TO EACH OTHER.

Glue

Fig. 2-32

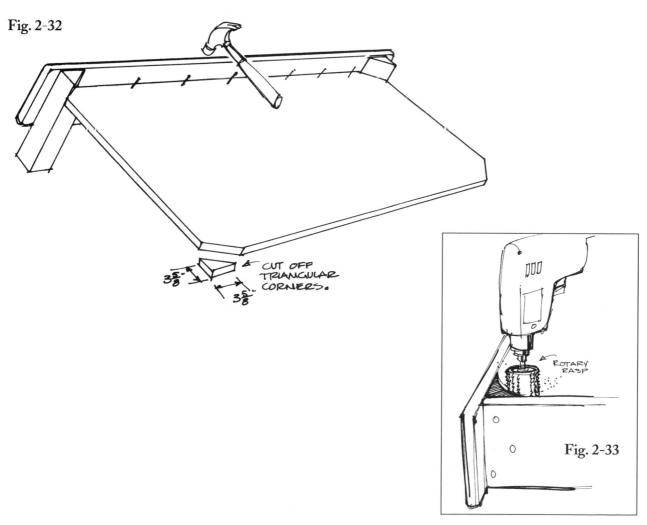

CUT OFF TRIANGULAR CORNERS.

3 5/8"

3 5/8"

ROTARY RASP

Fig. 2-33

LOFT BED

BY THE TIME CHILDREN REACH THE AGE of eight, the amount of available free room seems to diminish as toys, games, bikes and sleds start to take over. One of the best ways to improve this situation — as well as to create an exciting and welcome change for your child — is to build a loft bed. This creates an entirely new area that can be put to use as a living/play/work environment. A loft bed is also a good solution if a second child shares the same room, for both kids then have their own special place.

The loft bed is intended for an older child who feels comfortable climbing up and down a ladder and sleeping in a bunk bed arrangement. For an individual who wants more security, construct guard rails for the sides. The loft bed does not require the support of a wall, so you can install it anywhere in the room.

MATERIALS

Quantity	Size	Description	Location
2	4x8 sheets	¾-inch A/D or birch veneer plywood	bed platform, post brackets, pegs, side boards, end boards and stringers
4	10 feet	4x4 posts	corner posts
6	16 inches	2x6 clear pine	stair steps
1	30 inches	2x4 clear pine	rope post
2	40 inches	1x2 #2 pine	end platform supports
2	76 inches	1x2 #2 pine	side platform supports
1 quart		polyurethane	posts
1 quart		enamel paint	side and end boards, stairs
1	12 feet	1x4 clear pine	stair cleats
1 roll	2 inches wide	self-adhesive, nonskid tape	
32	1 inch	screw eyes	rope railing
1	25 feet	½-inch nylon rope	horizontal rope railing
1	150 feet	½-inch nylon rope	crisscrossed rope railing
8	6 inch	⅜-inch carriage bolts	post bolts
4	3 inch	⅜-inch carriage bolts, washers and nuts	rope post
8	6 inch	⅜-inch carriage bolts, washers and nuts	corner bolts
16	2 inch	drywall screws	ceiling brackets
1 box	1¼ inch	finishing nails	
4	1½ inch	#10 flathead screws	floor plug

OPTIONAL MATERIALS

Quantity	Size	Description	Location
2	47 inches	1x4 clear pine	end guard rails
2	63½ inches	1x4 clear pine	front and back guard rails
8	2 inch	#10 flathead screws	

As a child grows, the loft bed can inspire all kinds of activities. Our daughter strung a miniature hammock up to the rope railing at the end of her loft and put her stuffed animals to bed every night before she retired. She stuck glow-in-the-dark stars on the ceiling for star-gazing before dreaming and used the wall under the bed for a bulletin board.

To avoid having to make up the bed every day (which can be difficult while perching on a ladder), we use a nylon sleeping bag or a futon. Every week or so the sleeping bag or futon cover gets yanked off the bed and run through the washer and dryer.

Note that the same mattress precautions discussed with the child's bed also apply to this project.

Fig. 2-34

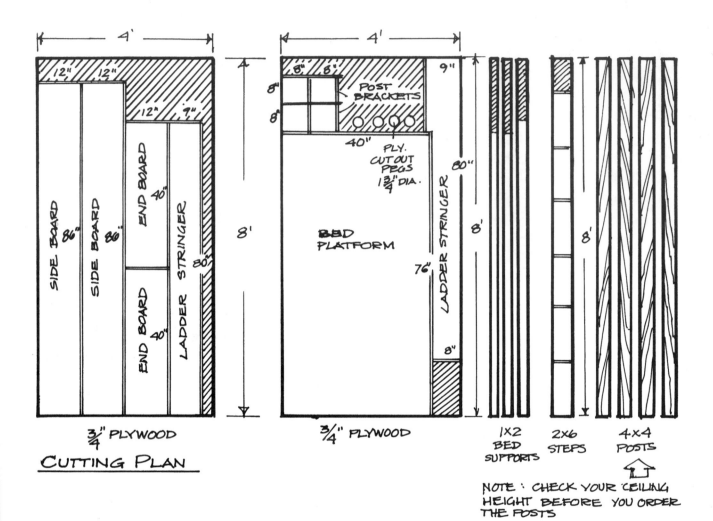

CUTTING PLAN

3/4" PLYWOOD

3/4" PLYWOOD

NOTE: CHECK YOUR CEILING HEIGHT BEFORE YOU ORDER THE POSTS

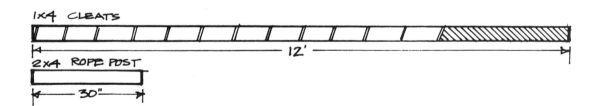

TO MAKE A DADO BY HAND

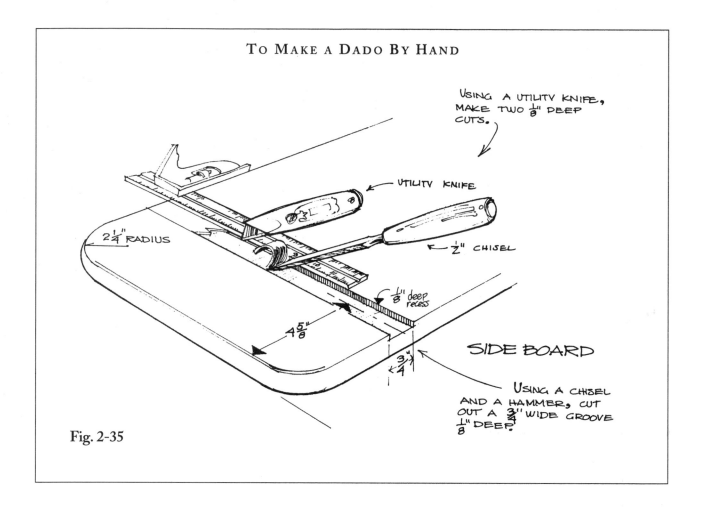

USING A UTILITY KNIFE, MAKE TWO $\frac{1}{8}$" DEEP CUTS.

UTILITY KNIFE

$\frac{1}{2}$" CHISEL

$2\frac{1}{4}$" RADIUS

$\frac{1}{8}$" deep recess

$4\frac{5}{8}$"

SIDE BOARD

$\frac{3}{4}$"

USING A CHISEL AND A HAMMER, CUT OUT A $\frac{3}{4}$" WIDE GROOVE $\frac{1}{8}$" DEEP.

Fig. 2-35

CORNER DETAIL

THIS TYPE OF JOINT IS GENERALLY FOUND ON HEAVY-DUTY TYPE CONSTRUCTION SUCH AS WORKBENCHES AND LOOMS. AS YOU CAN SEE, ONLY TWO BOLTS ARE NEEDED TO JOIN THE THREE PIECES TOGETHER. THESE TWO BOLTS MAKE A VERY STRONG JOINT AND AT THE SAME TIME ALLOW THE BED TO BE DISMANTLED AT A LATER DATE IN CASE YOU HAVE TO MOVE.

END BOARD

$2\frac{1}{2}$"

$1\frac{3}{4}$" THRU HOLES

$2\frac{1}{2}$"

$2\frac{1}{4}$ R. IF T.

$\frac{3}{8}$" DIA. HOLES

SIDE BOARD

$\frac{3}{8}$" × 6" CARRIAGE BOLTS

$4\frac{5}{8}$"

Fig. 2-36

6"

ROPE HOLE

$3\frac{1}{2}$"

$2\frac{1}{2}$"

6" CARRIAGE BOLT

END BOARD

12"

8"

$\frac{1}{8}$" RECESS INTO SIDE BOARD

$\frac{1}{2}$" PLYWOOD BED BOTTOM

$1\frac{3}{4}$ D. HOLE

7"

1×2 LEDGE

SECTION

$2\frac{3}{4}$" $\frac{3}{4}$"

4×4 POST

Fig. 2-37

Referring to the cutting plan (see Fig. 2-34), cut out all the plywood pieces. Pay particular attention to the one stringer that has a slight variation to it. Measure and mark four *Xs* on the floor to show where the posts will be positioned. The marks should form a rectangle that measures, from the center of each *X*, 76¾ inches by 43½ inches. Carefully measure the distance from the floor to the ceiling where each post will be placed and cut the posts ⅜ inch shorter than each measurement.

The posts are secured to the ceiling with 8-inch by 8-inch brackets. Cut out a 3½ inch by 3½ inch square opening from the center of each bracket so it will fit over the top of each post.

Referring to Figs. 2-36 and 2-37, make four 12-inch-long notches in the posts. This is where the side boards will be inserted and attached. To cut these notches, measure and mark a line 46 inches up from the bottom of each post. Then measure and mark another line 58 inches up from the bottom of each post. Chisel out a ¾-inch-deep notch between the two lines. Smooth the notch with a rasp.

The posts are anchored to the floor by positioning them over wooden plugs. Use a 1¾-inch hole saw to cut four 1¾-inch diameter plugs out of the scrap pieces of plywood. Drill a ⅛-inch pilot hole in the center of each plug (see Fig. 2-40). Screw the four plugs into the floor over the *Xs*. In the bottom center of each post, drill out a 1¾-inch diameter hole, ¾ inch deep (see Fig. 2-39).

Round off the four corners of the two side boards by scribing a 2¼-inch radius on them with a compass and using an electric jig saw to make the cuts. Smooth the edges with a rasp and sandpaper (see Fig. 2-64, page 99).

To join the end boards to the side boards, you must chisel out a dado on the ends of the side

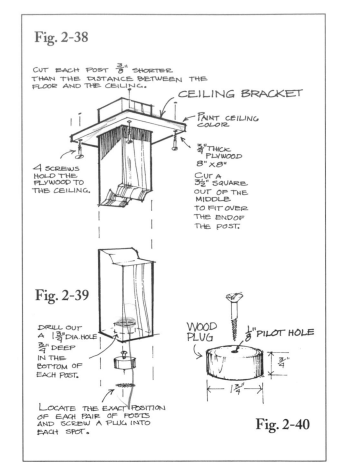

Fig. 2-38

CUT EACH POST ⅜" SHORTER THAN THE DISTANCE BETWEEN THE FLOOR AND THE CEILING.

CEILING BRACKET

PAINT CEILING COLOR

¾" THICK PLYWOOD 8" X 8"

CUT A 3½" SQUARE OUT OF THE MIDDLE TO FIT OVER THE END OF THE POST.

4 SCREWS HOLD THE PLYWOOD TO THE CEILING.

Fig. 2-39

DRILL OUT A 1¾" DIA. HOLE ¾" DEEP IN THE BOTTOM OF EACH POST.

LOCATE THE EXACT POSITION OF EACH PAIR OF POSTS AND SCREW A PLUG INTO EACH SPOT.

WOOD PLUG

⅛" PILOT HOLE

¾"

1¾"

Fig. 2-40

boards. Lay out each dado by marking a vertical line 4⅝-inches from the end of each side board. Use a utility knife, chisel and hammer to cut out a ⅛-inch-deep by ¾-inch-wide dado (see Fig. 2-35).

The side boards, end boards and posts are all joined together with carriage bolts. Only two 6-inch bolts are needed at each corner, which makes a very strong joint and at the same time allows the bed to be dismantled at a later date.

Through the side of each end board, drill two 1¾-inch diameter holes 2¾ inches from the end and 2½ inches from the top and the bottom of each board.

Through the ends of the same boards, carefully drill two ⅜-inch diameter holes 7 inches apart, so they bisect the center of the previously drilled 1¾-inch diameter holes (see Figs. 2-36 and 2-37).

Drill two ⅜-inch diameter holes 7 inches apart near both ends of each side board. The holes should be 4⅝ inches from the end of each side board and 2½ inches from the top and bottom.

On each post, measure and mark 2½ inches from the top and bottom of each notch. Make sure the marks are in the center of the post, then drill ½-inch diameter holes at the marks.

Begin assembling the two back posts, a side board and two end boards with four 6-inch carriage bolts by laying two of the posts down on the ground with the notches face up. Insert two bolts through the holes in each post. Fit the side piece into the notched posts so that the bolts extend through the holes in the side. Attach the two end pieces to the side piece so that the threaded ends of the bolts show through the 1¾-inch diameter holes in the

end boards (see Fig. 2-37). Loosely screw a ⅜-inch washer and nut onto the end of the bolt. Don't tighten the bolts until the entire structure is in place. Slide a bracket over the top of each post.

Align the posts over the plugs on the floor and raise the section until it is vertical (see Fig. 2-41). Have someone hold it in place while you assemble the two other posts and side board and slide the ceiling brackets onto the posts. Raise this second section to meet the one already standing and position the posts over the plugs in the floor. Bolt the front side piece and the front posts to the end boards. Check to see whether the posts are squarely aligned by measuring diagonally between the posts (they should be the same). Make any necessary adjustments until the measurements agree. Tighten up the carriage bolts. Screw the ceiling brackets into the ceiling using #10 2-inch drywall screws.

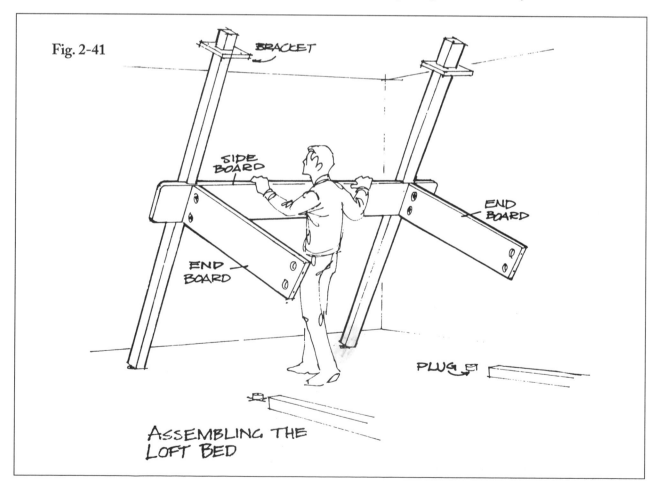

Fig. 2-41

BRACKET

SIDE BOARD

END BOARD

END BOARD

PLUG

ASSEMBLING THE LOFT BED

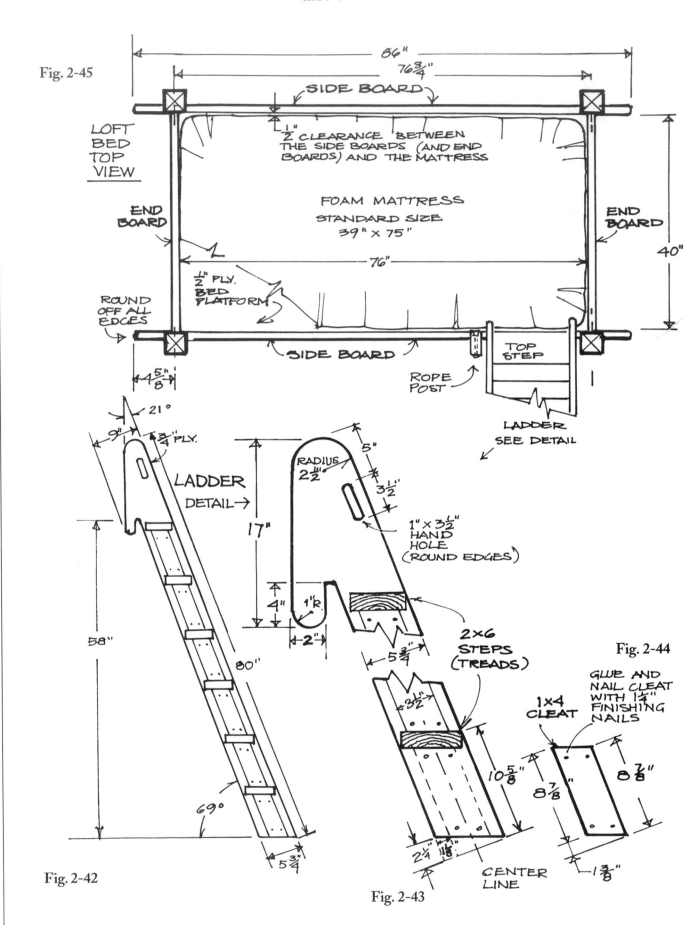

Fig. 2-45

LOFT
BED
TOP
VIEW

86"

76¾"

SIDE BOARD

½" CLEARANCE BETWEEN
THE SIDE BOARDS (AND END
BOARDS) AND THE MATTRESS

FOAM MATTRESS
STANDARD SIZE
39" X 75"

END
BOARD

END
BOARD

40"

76"

½" PLY.
BED
PLATFORM

ROUND
OFF ALL
EDGES

SIDE BOARD

TOP
STEP

ROPE
POST

LADDER
SEE DETAIL

4⅝"

21°

9"

¾" PLY.

LADDER
DETAIL →

RADIUS
2½"

5"

3½"

1" X 3½"
HAND
HOLE
(ROUND EDGES)

17"

4"

1" R.

2x6
STEPS
(TREADS)

Fig. 2-44

58"

80"

2"

5¾"

3½"

GLUE AND
NAIL CLEAT
WITH 1¼"
FINISHING
NAILS

1x4
CLEAT

8⅞"

10⅝"

8⅞"

69°

5¾"

2¼" 1⅛"

CENTER
LINE

1⅜"

Fig. 2-42

Fig. 2-43

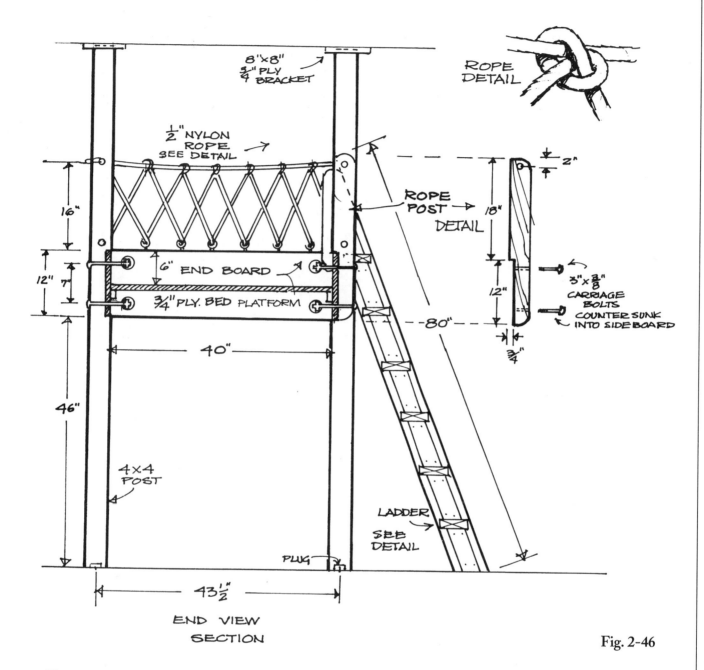

ROPE DETAIL

8"×8"
¾" PLY
BRACKET

½" NYLON
ROPE
SEE DETAIL

16"

12"

7"

6" END BOARD

¾" PLY. BED PLATFORM

40"

46"

4×4
POST

PLUG

43½"

**END VIEW
SECTION**

ROPE
POST → DETAIL

18"

12"

2"

80"

¾"

3"×⅜"
CARRIAGE
BOLTS
COUNTER SUNK
INTO SIDE BOARD

LADDER
SEE DETAIL

Fig. 2-46

To provide a ledge to support the bed board, screw the four pieces of #2 pine 1x2 to the side and end boards, measuring 8 inches down from the top of the boards and driving the screws every 4 inches. Lay the plywood bed platform on top of the ledge and attach the platform to the ledge by drilling in screws at an angle every 4 inches.

To create a smooth finish that can be easily cleaned, sand and paint the posts with three coats of polyurethane. The plywood sides and end boards

can either be covered with three coats of polyurethane or painted with a bright enamel color. If you use birch veneer plywood, you may want to let the wood show through and finish all the surfaces with polyurethane.

The ladder is composed of two stringers and six steps or treads. The steps are supported by 1x4 cleats that are glued and nailed to the interior of the stringers. The top of the ladder hooks onto the side edge of the bed and must be finished according to

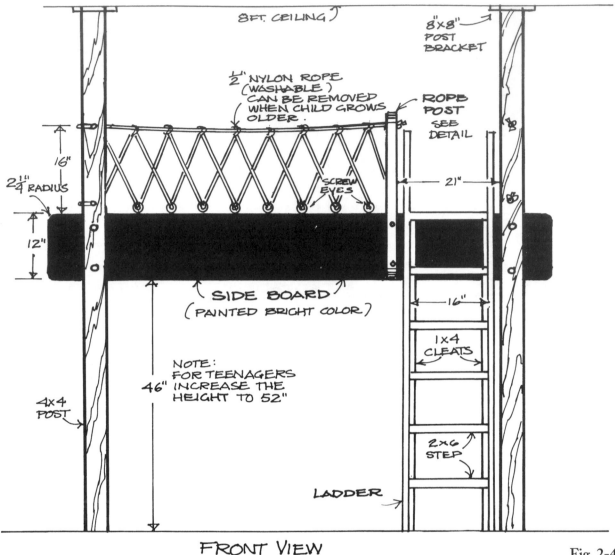

FRONT VIEW

Fig. 2-47

the shape and dimensions shown in Figs. 2-42 and 2-43. Because the ladder leans against the bed at a slant, the bottom of the stringers must be cut at 69 degrees using a protractor. To do this, measure 2¼ inches up from the bottom of the back edge of one of the stringers and draw a line from this point down to the front bottom corner of the stringer. Saw off this triangular wedge (see Fig. 2-43). Repeat with the other stringer.

Hook the stringers over the side of the bed. To show where the top of the steps go, make a mark every 10⅝ inches on the front and rear edges of

each stringer, starting from the bottom. Draw a line across the interior side of each stringer connecting these front and rear marks. After both stringers are marked, lay them side by side to make sure that the lines coincide and to ensure that the steps will be level.

Cut six 14½-inch-long steps from the 8-foot-long 2x6; make certain that each step is exactly the same length. The cleats are cut out of the 12-foot-long 1x4. Measure 1⅛ inches up from the bottom edge of the 1x4 and draw a line from this point down to the opposite bottom corner. Saw off this wedge-shaped piece of wood. Measure 8⅞ inches up from each bottom corner and make a mark. Connect the two marks with a line and saw across this line; you now have a cleat. Use this first cleat as a pattern to cut the remaining eleven cleats (see Fig. 2-44).

Glue and nail — with four 1¼-inch finishing nails — the bottom cleat for each stringer, placing them flush with the bottom of the stringers (see Fig. 2-43). Make sure the cleats are centered so that they are 1⅛ inches from the front and back of the stringers.

Lay one of the steps on top of the cleats and glue and nail it in place with 1¼-inch finishing nails. Repeat the cleat and step construction process until all six steps and twelve cleats are attached to the stringers. Sand and cover with three coats of polyurethane. To make the steps more skid-proof, apply nonskid tape to the tops of each step.

For a nautical look, string a rope railing between the bed posts on each side. To support the rope where it meets the ladder, bolt a post support to the side of the bed. To construct this rope post, cut the 30-inch-long 2x4 and round off its top using an electric jig saw. Cut a ¾-inch by 12-inch notch out of the lower end of the post and drill two ⅜-inch diameter holes 2 inches from the bottom and top of the notch (see Fig. 2-46).

Place the post 21 inches to the left of the corner post. While holding it in position and using the existing post holes as a guide, drill through the post holes and the side board. Bolt the post onto the bed using carriage bolts that are 3 inches long and ⅜ inch wide.

Drill four ¾-inch diameter cross holes through each of the four corner posts with two of the holes drilled through one side and two of the holes drilled on another side, perpendicular to the first holes.

The holes drilled parallel to the length of the sides should be located 16 inches and 2 inches above the side boards. So that the holes drilled parallel to the width of the bed do not intersect them, you should drill the second set of holes slightly lower—14½ inches and 1½ inches above the side boards. Screw ¼-inch by 3-inch screw eyes spaced every 6 inches into the top edge of the side and end boards (see Figs. 2-46 or 2-47).

To make the rope railing, thread the 25-foot-long rope through the top hole in the post support to the left of the ladder, knotting it at the end (see Fig. 2-47). Continue threading the rope counterclockwise through the top holes in the four posts. When you reach the post to the right side of the ladder, pull the rope tight and knot it.

Make a knot at the end of the second piece of rope and thread the free end through the lower hole in the rope post. Continuing in a counterclockwise direction, lace this rope to the top rope using overhand knots (see detail, Fig. 2-46) and then back down through the screw eyes, making a zigzag pattern. When the rope reaches the post to the right side of the ladder, pull it tight and knot it. Don't cut off the loose ends until you are satisfied with the railing.

For additional security, construct guard rails on any sides of the bed that are not against the wall. The U.S. Consumer Product Safety Commission recommends allowing a space of 3½ inches or less between the bottom of bunk bed guard rails and the top of the side and end boards. On the front side of the bed, screw the 1x4 clear pine guard rail to the inside of the two corner posts. On the ends of the bed, screw the guard rails to the outside of the end posts.

Finally, lay a standard twin-sized (39 inches by 75 inches) mattress on the bed platform and the loft bed is ready to use.

CHAIRS AND TABLES

STORAGE BENCH

THE STORAGE BENCH IS A POPULAR piece of furniture and one that is relatively easy to build. It contains two large drawers (or open shelves, if you don't want to bother making drawers) and is on casters, so it can easily be moved from place to place.

Our daughter usually kept her storage bench under her loft bed and used it as a cozy reading nook. It also looks attractive at the foot of a bed and makes a comfortable place for a child to sit while tying shoelaces, watching a video or visiting with a special friend. For a more comfortable seat, make a cushion out of foam and cover it with a bright print fabric.

MATERIALS

Quantity	Size	Description	Location
1	4x4 sheet	¾-inch birch veneer plywood	sides
1	4x8 sheet	½-inch birch veneer plywood	top, bottom, center divider and back
1 pint		polyurethane or bright enamel paint	wooden surfaces
1	17 inch by 36 inch	2-inch-thick foam	cushion
1 yard		fabric	cushion
4	2 inch	casters (stem type)	

OPTIONAL MATERIALS

Quantity	Size	Description	Location
1	4x4 sheet	¾-inch birch veneer plywood	drawer fronts
1	4x8 sheet	½-inch birch veneer plywood	drawer sides and backs
1	4x4 sheet	¼-inch masonite hardboard	drawer bottoms
1	6 feet	¾-inch by ¼-inch pine molding	cleats
2	3 inch	chrome wire pulls	drawer fronts
1 box	1½ inch	finishing nails	

Referring to the cutting plan (see Fig. 2-48), cut out all the pieces. Be especially careful when cutting the center divider; it must be absolutely square and accurate to within ¹⁄₁₆ inch.

Assemble the pieces without glue to see if they all fit together accurately. Lay the bottom piece down and mark a center line, measuring 18 inches from each side (see Fig. 2-49). Draw two ¼-inch lines on either side of the center line to indicate where the center divider should be placed. Do the same for the top piece. Glue the back piece to the bottom piece and the center divider to the bottom and back pieces. After the glue has dried, apply glue to the top of the center divider and the top edge of the back and place the top piece on the back piece and center divider. Apply glue to the edges of the top, back and bottom pieces where they will meet the sides and attach the two side pieces with 1½-inch finishing nails. Nail 1½-inch finishing nails every 2 inches along a center line in the top where it joins the center divider (see Fig. 2-49). Round off the edges of the side pieces using an electric jig saw and sand everything smooth.

Using a spade bit, drill holes for the casters in the bottom edge of the side pieces 2½ inches from the exterior edges of the sides. Generally, casters take a ⅜-inch hole, but check the directions on the package to confirm the size. Set the casters in the holes.

Finish the storage bench with three coats of polyurethane or enamel paint. For details on making the drawers, see Fig. 2-51 and pages 28–33. If you wish, you can disregard the drawers and leave the shelf open.

CUTTING PLAN

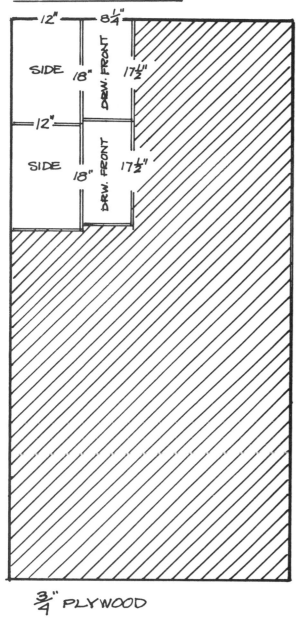

SIDE

12"

8¼"

DRW. FRONT

18"

17½"

SIDE

12"

DRW. FRONT

18"

17½"

¾" PLYWOOD

Fig. 2-48

8½"

17"

14¾"

7¾"

BACK

36"

TOP

36"

BOTTOM

DRW. SIDE

15¼"

7¾"

DRW. SIDE

15¼"

7¾"

DRW. SIDE

15¼"

7¾"

DRW. SIDE

15¼"

7¾"

DRW. BACK

17¼"

7¾"

DRAWER BACK

17¼"

15½"

CENTER DIVIDER

8"

½" PLYWOOD

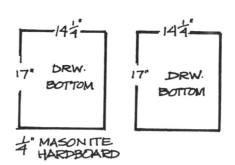

14¼"

17"

DRW. BOTTOM

14¼"

17"

DRW. BOTTOM

¼" MASONITE HARDBOARD

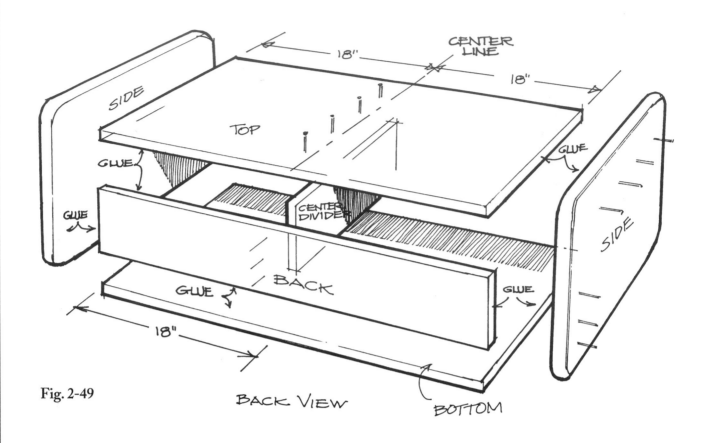

SIDE

18"

CENTER LINE

18"

GLUE

TOP

GLUE

GLUE

CENTER DIVIDER

SIDE

GLUE

BACK

GLUE

Fig. 2-49

18"

BACK VIEW

BOTTOM

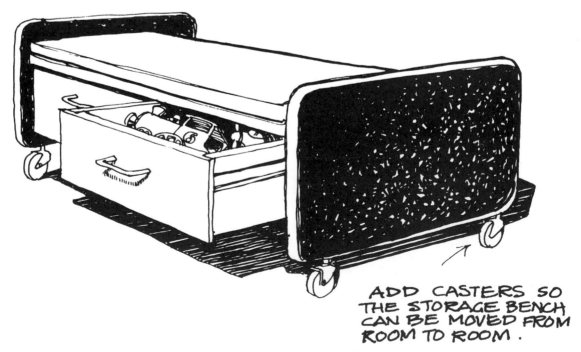

ADD CASTERS SO THE STORAGE BENCH CAN BE MOVED FROM ROOM TO ROOM.

Fig. 2-50

Fig. 2-51

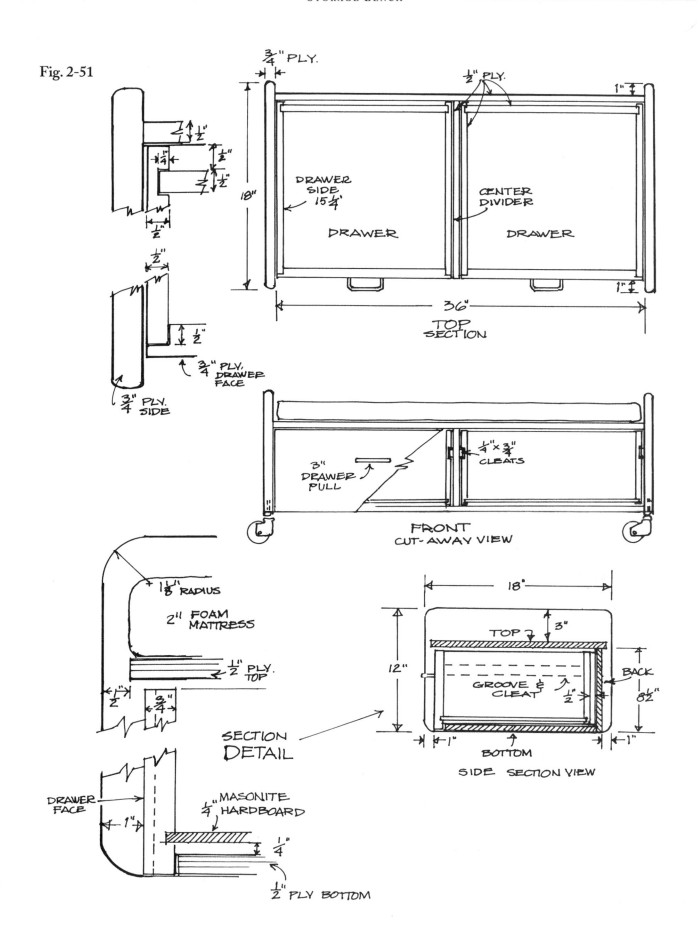

$\frac{3}{4}$" PLY.

$\frac{1}{2}$" PLY.

1"

$\frac{1}{2}$"

$\frac{1}{4}$"

$\frac{1}{2}$"

$\frac{1}{2}$"

18"

DRAWER SIDE 15$\frac{1}{4}$'

CENTER DIVIDER

DRAWER

DRAWER

1"

36"

TOP SECTION

$\frac{1}{2}$"

$\frac{1}{2}$"

$\frac{3}{4}$" PLY. DRAWER FACE

$\frac{3}{4}$" PLY. SIDE

3" DRAWER PULL

$\frac{1}{4}$" x $\frac{3}{4}$" CLEATS

FRONT
CUT-AWAY VIEW

1$\frac{1}{8}$" RADIUS

2" FOAM MATTRESS

$\frac{1}{2}$" PLY. TOP

$\frac{1}{2}$"

$\frac{3}{4}$"

SECTION DETAIL

18"

TOP

3"

12"

GROOVE & CLEAT

$\frac{1}{2}$"

BACK

8$\frac{1}{2}$"

1"

BOTTOM

1"

SIDE SECTION VIEW

DRAWER FACE

1"

$\frac{1}{4}$" MASONITE HARDBOARD

$\frac{1}{4}$"

$\frac{1}{2}$" PLY BOTTOM

ADJUST-TABLE

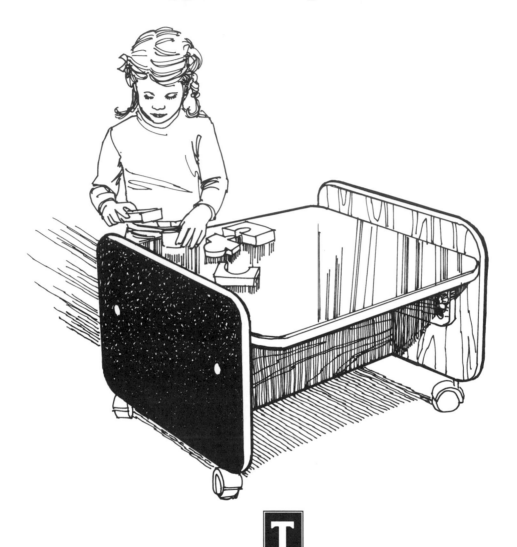

THE ADJUST-TABLE IS SIMPLE TO MAKE and can be completed in just one day. It is comprised of two basic parts: the base and the table top. As the name implies, this table is adjustable. By simply unscrewing four wing nuts (no tools necessary) and repositioning them in a different set of holes, the table height can be raised or lowered to accommodate kids from ages two to six. It rests on freewheeling casters for maximum portability, and the surface of the table is covered with a sheet of plexiglas, which can be removed and cleaned.

The table functions not only as a children's dining table but also as a work table for making cookies, building clay monsters or drawing pictures. It is appropriate for practically any sort of sit-down activity or skill. After your child outgrows it, the adjust-table can be moved to the living room and used as a side table.

MATERIALS

Quantity	Size	Description	Location
1	4x4 sheet	¾-inch plywood or melamine	top, sides, brackets and center divider
1	2 feet by 2 feet	⅛-inch white acrylic plexiglas	table-top surface
1 box	2 inch	finishing nails	
4	2 inch	⅜-inch carriage bolts and washers	table sides
4		⅜-inch wing nuts	table sides
4	2 inch	casters (stem type)	
1 pint		polyurethane	wooden surfaces
1 pint		enamel paint	wooden surfaces

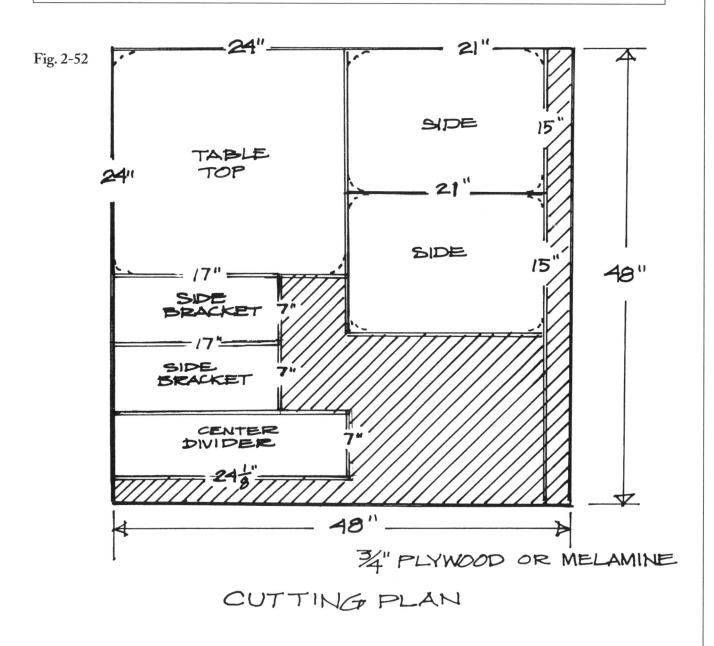

Fig. 2-52

¾" PLYWOOD OR MELAMINE

CUTTING PLAN

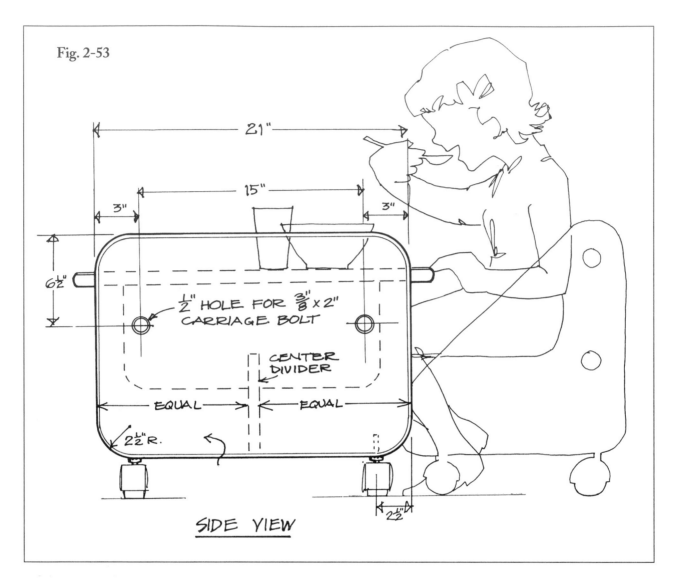

Fig. 2-53

SIDE VIEW

Referring to the cutting plan (see Fig. 2-52), cut out all the pieces. Note that the radius for the table top and side pieces are different. To round off the corners, use a compass to mark off a 2½-inch radius on the side pieces (see Fig. 2-53) and a 1½-inch radius on the table top (see Fig. 2-54). Then cut along the marked corners with an electric jig saw.

Referring to Fig. 2-56, cut a slot ¾ inch wide and 5½ inches high in each side bracket. Drill four ⅜-inch diameter holes at both ends of each bracket and 1¼ inches from each side, making sure that the two rows of holes are 15 inches apart.

Apply glue to the top edge of each bracket and attach to the underneath edge of the table top. Make sure the side of each bracket is at right angles to and flush with the outside edge of the table top. After the glue has dried, reinforce with finishing nails every 2 inches (see Fig. 2-57).

Using a ½-inch spade bit, drill two holes for the carriage bolts in each side piece (see Figs. 2-53 and 2-55). Position the holes 15 inches apart, 6½ inches down from the top edge of the table side and 3 inches in from the side edge of the table side. It is essential that the bracket holes and the side holes are each 15 inches apart, so they will line up when repositioning the table.

Fig. 2-54

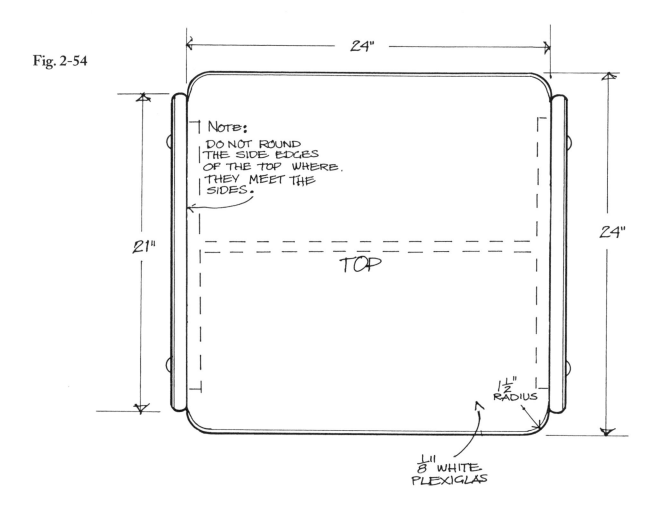

24"

21"

24"

NOTE:

DO NOT ROUND
THE SIDE EDGES
OF THE TOP WHERE
THEY MEET THE
SIDES.

TOP

1½" RADIUS

⅛" WHITE PLEXIGLAS

Fig. 2-55

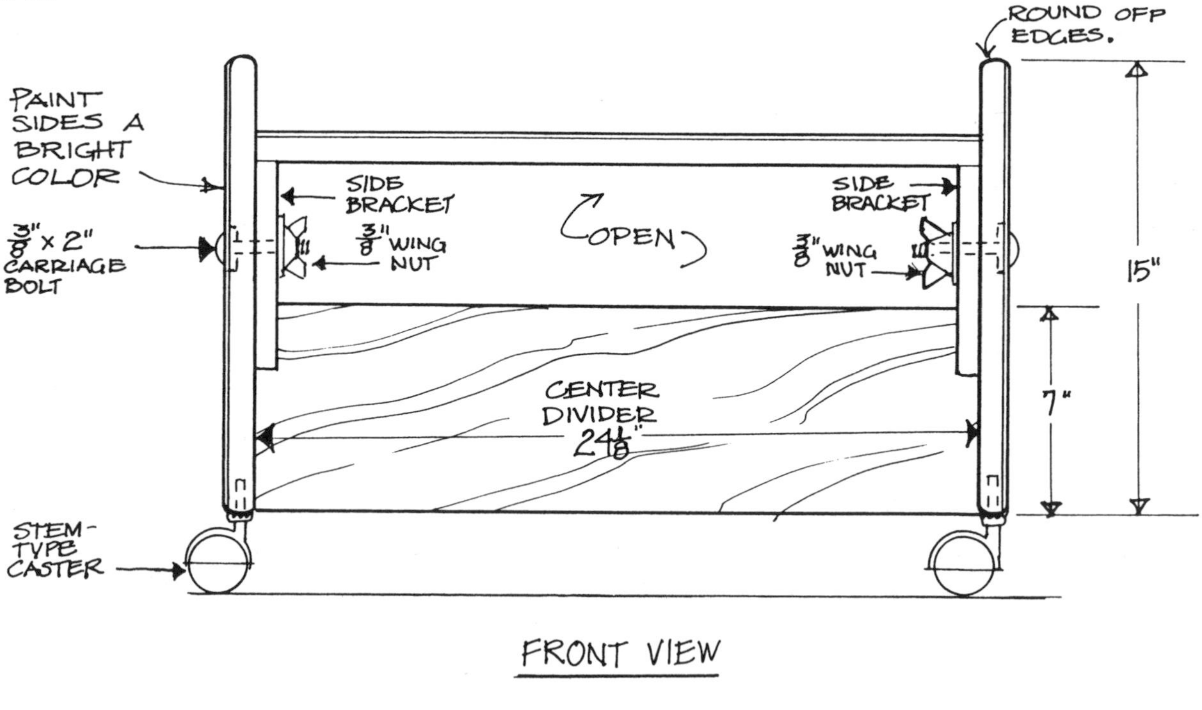

PAINT
SIDES A
BRIGHT
COLOR

⅜" X 2"
CARRIAGE
BOLT

SIDE BRACKET

⅜" WING NUT

OPEN

SIDE BRACKET

⅜" WING NUT

ROUND OFF EDGES.

15"

7"

CENTER DIVIDER
24⅛"

STEM-TYPE CASTER

FRONT VIEW

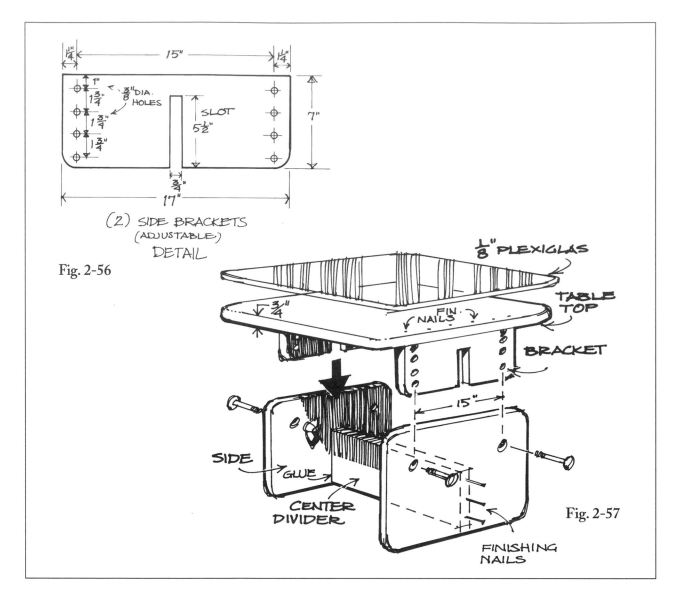

(2) SIDE BRACKETS
(ADJUSTABLE)
DETAIL

Fig. 2-56

Fig. 2-57

Using a combination square (see Fig. 2-59, page 97), find the inside center of each side piece, mark with a pencil and glue the side pieces to the ends of the center divider (see Fig. 2-57). After the glue is dry, reinforce with finishing nails every 2 inches. Slide the slots in the brackets over the center divider, completing the table assembly.

Using an electric jig saw with a fine blade and set at a slow speed, round off the corners of the plexiglas. Round off and sand the edges of the table top and the two side pieces (see page 26). Note that the side edges of the top and side pieces are not rounded where they meet (see Fig. 2-54).

With a spade bit, drill holes for the casters 2½ inches from the outside edges of the table sides. Generally, casters take a ⅜-inch hole, but check the directions on the package to confirm the size. Set the casters in the holes.

Paint all exposed wood surfaces with polyurethane and/or enamel paint. Adjust the table to the desired height by lining up the appropriate bracket holes with the side holes. Place the four carriage bolts through the holes — from the outside in — and secure them with washers and wing nuts (see Fig. 2-55).

STORAGE CHAIR

THE STORAGE CHAIR IS BOTH A CHAIR and a toy. Children enjoy pushing it around the house and can use it as a storage cart as they pick up their toys. After a baby masters standing up, this chair also helps when learning how to walk. Babies can steady themselves by holding onto the top rail and gradually progress from there until they are then able to walk. Make sure the chair is on a carpet or heavy pile rug, however, as it might roll too quickly on a hard floor.

MATERIALS

Quantity	Size	Description	Location
1	4x4 sheet	¾-inch plywood	backrest, back, front, sides, seat and bottom
1	30 inches	1-inch dia. wooden dowel	hinge dowel for seat and stationary dowel
4	2 inch	twin-wheel casters (stem type)	
1 box	2 inch	finishing nails	
1 pint		polyurethane	
1 pint		enamel paint	

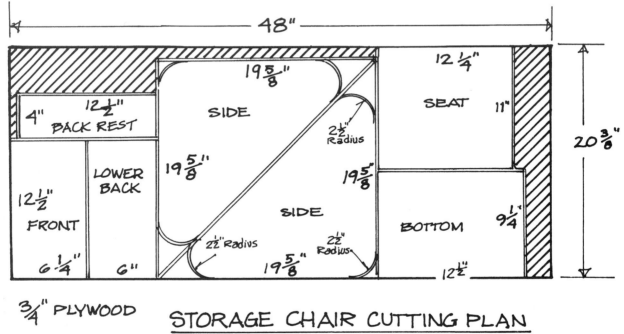

STORAGE CHAIR CUTTING PLAN

Fig. 2-58

Cut out the plywood pieces according to the cutting plan (see Fig. 2-58). Gently round off the two front corners of the chair seat with an electric jig saw. To round off the triangular corners of the two sides, use a compass to draw a 2½-inch radius on all six corners. Carefully cut off the corners with the electric jig saw.

Using the same compass pivot point (2½-inch radius) and a 1-inch spade bit, drill a 1-inch hole in the top of both sides (see Fig. 2-60 and 2-63). This is where the stationary dowel will go.

Drill another 1-inch hole in both sides, positioning it 6¾ inches from the bottom and 2½ inches from the edge of the side. These holes hold a dowel that becomes a hinge for the seat.

Cut the 1-inch diameter wooden dowel in half, creating two 15-inch-long pieces. To make the hinge dowel, use a rasp to flatten one side of the dowel so that it will fit flat against the back edge of the seat. Leave 1⅜ inches on both ends of the dowel rounded (see Fig. 2-62). Glue and nail with 2-inch finishing nails.

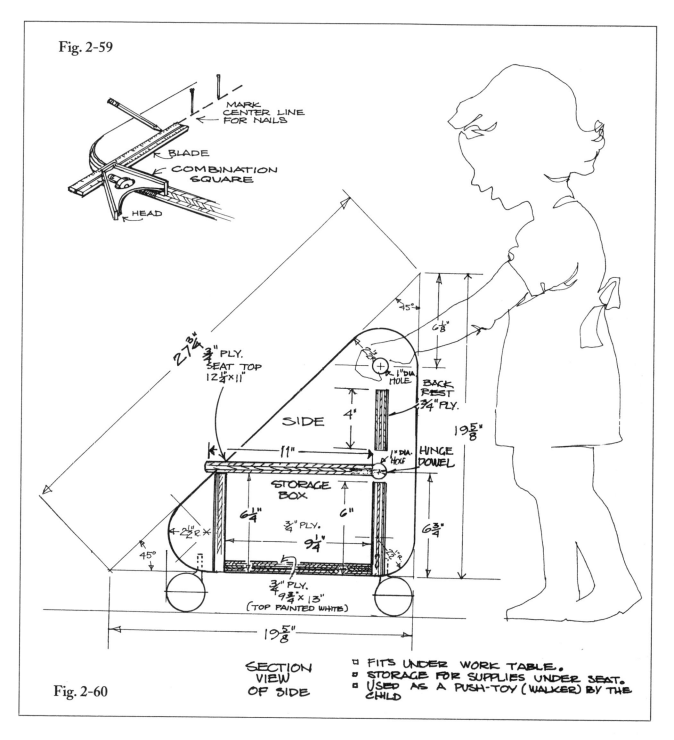

Fig. 2-59

MARK
CENTER LINE
FOR NAILS

BLADE

COMBINATION
SQUARE

HEAD

27¾"

¾" PLY.
SEAT TOP
12¼"×11"

45°

6⅛"

2½"

1" DIA.
HOLE

BACK
REST
¾" PLY.

19⅝"

SIDE

4"

11"

1" DIA.
HOLE

HINGE
DOWEL

STORAGE
BOX

6¼"

6"

¾" PLY.

9¼"

6¾"

2½"R.×

45°

2½"

¾" PLY.
9¾"×13"
(TOP PAINTED WHITE)

19⅝"

Fig. 2-60

SECTION
VIEW
OF SIDE

▫ FITS UNDER WORK TABLE.
▫ STORAGE FOR SUPPLIES UNDER SEAT.
▫ USED AS A PUSH-TOY (WALKER) BY THE CHILD

To assemble the chair, begin by gluing and nailing together the front and back pieces flush to the bottom of the chair (see Fig. 2-63). This forms the storage box under the chair seat. Draw a pencil line parallel to and 2⅛ inches from the back edge of each chair side to mark where the storage box and the back rest will be glued to the two chair sides.

Lay one side face down and flat on the floor or worktable. Using the pencil line as your guide, glue the storage box to the side; make sure that the bottom edges are flush (see Fig. 2-63).

After the glue is dry, insert the hinge dowel into the 1-inch hole in the side of the chair but do not

Fig. 2-61

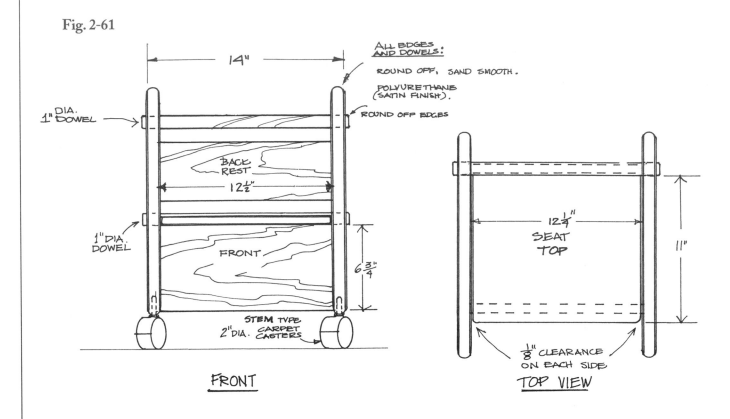

ALL EDGES
AND DOWELS:

ROUND OFF, SAND SMOOTH.

POLYURETHANE
(SATIN FINISH).

ROUND OFF EDGES

14"

1" DIA.
1" DOWEL

BACK
REST

12½"

1" DIA.
DOWEL

FRONT

6¾"

STEM TYPE
2" DIA. CARPET CASTERS

FRONT

12¼"
SEAT
TOP

11"

⅛" CLEARANCE
ON EACH SIDE

TOP VIEW

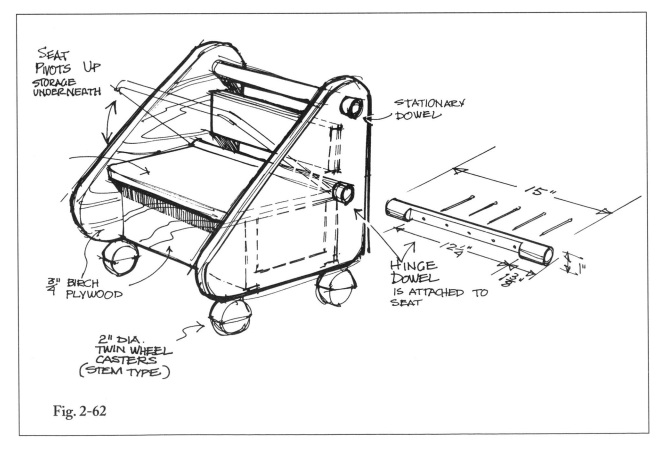

SEAT
PIVOTS UP
STORAGE
UNDERNEATH

STATIONARY
DOWEL

¾" BIRCH
PLYWOOD

HINGE
DOWEL
IS ATTACHED TO
SEAT

15"

12¼"

1"

1¾"

2" DIA.
TWIN WHEEL
CASTERS
(STEM TYPE)

Fig. 2-62

Fig. 2-63

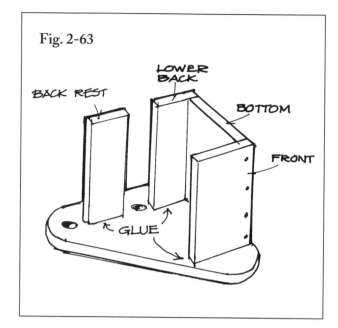

apply any glue to the dowel. Allow the dowel to protrude slightly from the hole.

Using the same parallel pencil line as your guide, glue on the back rest ¾ inch above the hinge dowel so that the chair seat can be lifted easily. After the glue on the back rest is dry, glue the second side to the chair using the pencil marks as your guide. Push the hinge dowel into and through the other side hole so the dowel protrudes slightly from both ends (see Fig. 2-61). Use a combination square to mark where the finishing nails will go. Place the handle or head of the square along the bottom edge of the chair and the metal blade flat against the chair side (see Fig. 2-59). Nail in finishing nails every 2 inches. Slide the other piece of dowel through the

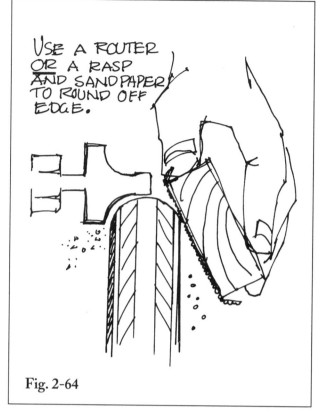

USE A ROUTER OR A RASP AND SANDPAPER TO ROUND OFF EDGE.

Fig. 2-64

top holes in the sides and glue in place. Round off all the edges (see Fig. 2-64), sand smooth and finish with polyurethane and/or enamel paint.

Using a spade bit, drill holes for the casters ½ inch from the front and back edges of the storage box (see Figs. 2-60 and 2-61). Generally, casters take a ⅜-inch hole, but check the directions on the package to confirm the size. Set the casters in the holes. You might consider using casters with a built-in adjustable brake (see Fig. 2-99, page 133).

WORK

CHILD'S ART DESK

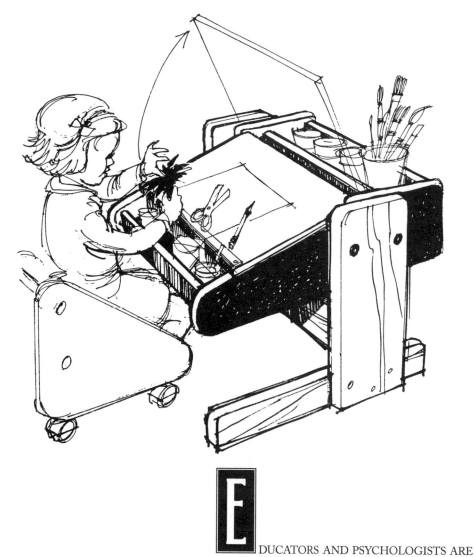

EDUCATORS AND PSYCHOLOGISTS ARE becoming increasingly aware that artistic development helps children to become "artists" and teaches them how to look at and interpret the world from another perspective. Drawing and painting, for example, aid a child in the coordination and development of small motor skills and are a learning tool in discovering colors, shapes and textures.

Besides being a valuable asset to a child's intellectual growth and artistic development, the art desk is also useful in providing many hours of quiet time during which parents can get some of their own work done.

One of the best features of the art desk is the opportunity to use practically endless rolls of drawing paper. A roll fits through a slot at the top and under a tear-off bar at the bottom of the drawing board. When finished drawing, the child can tear off the paper by pulling it up and across the bar — there's no need to call mom or dad. The paper tear-off bar also prevents crayons, pencils or scissors from sliding off the board.

MATERIALS

Quantity	Size	Description	Location
1	4 feet	2x4 clear pine	legs
1	4 feet	⁵⁄₄x8 clear pine	uprights
1	4x4 sheet	½-inch birch veneer plywood	bottom, desk top, sides, center divider, paper holder and storage compartments
1	3 feet	½-inch dia. wood dowel	paper holder
1	2 feet	⅛-inch by 1-inch aluminum bar	paper tear-off bar
4	3 inch	⅜-inch carriage bolts and washers	uprights and sides
6	2½ inch	#10 flathead screws	uprights
1	16 inches by 24 inches	⅛-inch white acrylic plexiglas	desk top
4	1 inch	nylon glide tacks	
1	18 inches wide	roll of white paper	desk holder
1 box	2 inch	finishing nails	
1 pint		polyurethane or enamel paint	

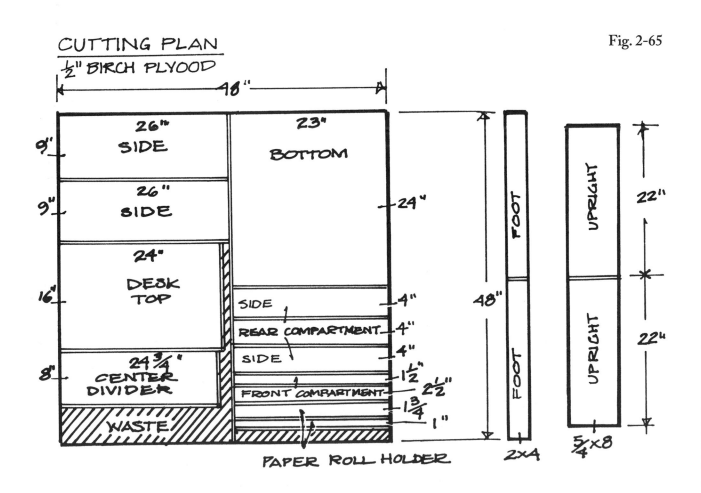

CUTTING PLAN
½" BIRCH PLYOOD

Fig. 2-65

The front compartment of the desk holds small poster-paint bottles, paste, scissors, crayons or other art materials. The rear compartment stores items that are used less frequently: markers, various brushes, colored pencils. Plastic flowerpots make convenient and colorful holders for these items. A worthwhile investment is a small clamping lamp with a 75-watt bulb so you can be sure your child has plenty of light.

Where do you keep a child's finished artwork after it has been admired and shown to friends and relatives? In the child's art desk, of course, under the lift-up desktop. As the drawings begin to accumulate, your child can be encouraged to clean out the desk — a chore many adults find difficult — and throw away old drawings to make room for new ones.

As your child grows, the art desk can be adjusted by removing the four bolts on the sides, lifting the table up until the next set of holes lines up and inserting the bolts in their new location. Note that the three sets of holes are in the side of the desk itself, not in the pedestal.

This art desk is fairly easy to construct and shouldn't take more than a couple of weekends. Referring to the cutting plan (see Fig. 2-65), cut out all the pieces. Use an electric jig saw to cut the side pieces to the shape indicated in Fig. 2-68.

Drill a hole in each side with a ½-inch spade bit, ⅝ inch from the top edge to accept the wooden hinge dowel. Using an electric jig saw, notch out the corners on the desk top ¾ inch from the edges (see detail in Fig. 2-67).

To make the hinge dowel, use a rasp to flatten one side of the dowel so it will lay flat against the edge of the desk top. Leave ¾ inch on each end of the dowel rounded. Glue and nail the dowel to the desktop (see Fig. 2-67 and detail in Fig. 2-73).

While the glue on the hinge is drying, round off the top edges and sand until smooth the two front compartment pieces, the paper roll holder and the three rear compartment pieces. Assemble the rear compartment by nailing the sides to the bottom with 2-inch finishing nails. Stand the bottom piece up on edge (see Fig. 2-71) and, using the front and rear compartment pieces as temporary supports, glue and nail one of the side pieces for the desk to the edge of the bottom piece. Remember to make the edge of the side flush with the bottom.

Turn the desk over so the newly attached side is face down on the workbench or floor. Glue one end of the paper holder and the two storage compartments to the side (see Figs. 2-70 and 2-73). Slide one end of the hinge dowel through the ½-inch hinge hole in the side piece. Note that the base of the front storage compartment and the paper holder is the bottom of the desk. Place glue on the other ends of the storage compartment and the paper holder and attach the second side to the ends, fitting the exposed dowel end through the ½-inch side hole. Check for squareness and nail 2-inch finishing nails where pieces are glued together.

The pedestal that holds the art desk consists of two feet and two uprights connected by a center divider. Draw a line down the inside center of both uprights. Chisel out each ¾-inch-wide by ¼-inch-deep by 8-inch-long groove, starting 3½ inches up from the bottom center of each upright, to accept the center dividers (see Fig. 2-69). This is where the center divider will go. Make a rabbet across the grain ½ inch deep by 3½ inches long out of the inside bottom edge of both uprights in order to accept the 2x4 feet. Split out the wood with a hammer and chisel. Finish off the notch with a rasp.

Place the 2x4 feet in position and screw them in place (see Fig. 2-73). Fit the center divider into the grooves of the two uprights. Glue and then screw the uprights to the divider using #10 2½-inch flat-

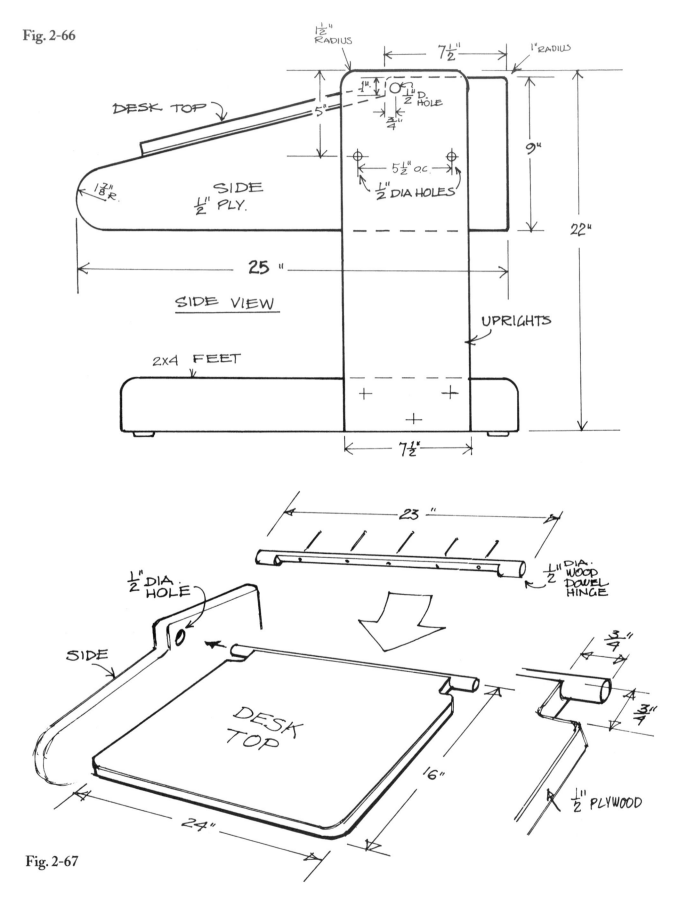

Fig. 2-66

DESK TOP

SIDE
½" PLY.

SIDE VIEW

1½"
RADIUS

1" RADIUS

7½"

9"

22"

1"

½" D. HOLE

¾"

5½" O.C.

½" DIA HOLES

5"

1⅞" R.

25"

2x4 FEET

UPRIGHTS

7½"

23"

½" DIA. WOOD DOWEL HINGE

½" DIA. HOLE

SIDE

DESK TOP

16"

24"

¾"

¾"

¾"

½" PLYWOOD

Fig. 2-67

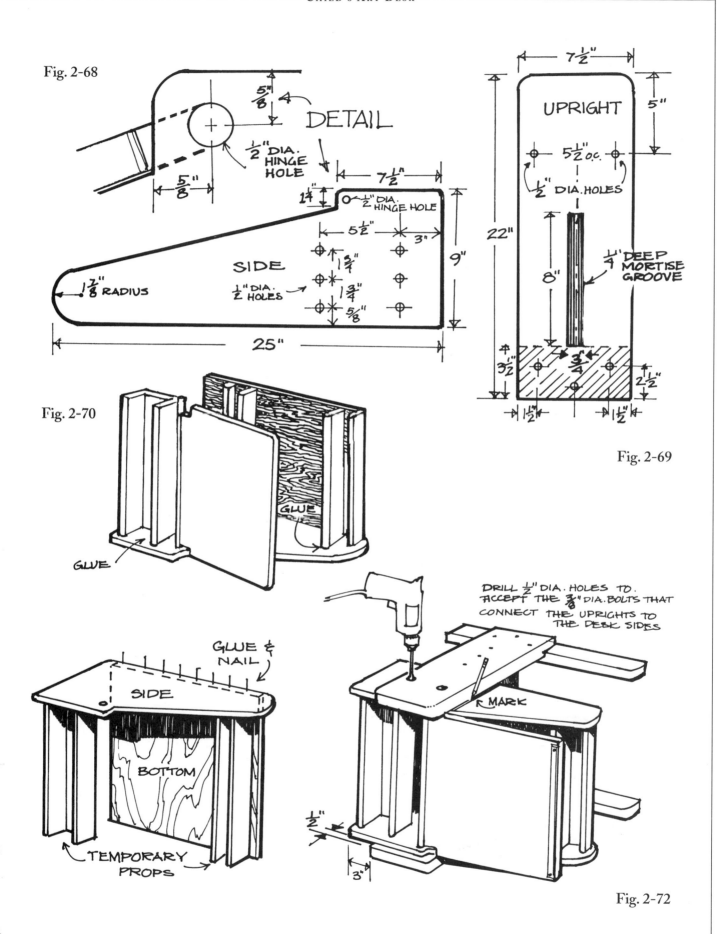

Fig. 2-68

DETAIL

$\frac{5}{8}$"

$\frac{1}{2}$" DIA. HINGE HOLE

$\frac{5}{8}$"

$1\frac{1}{4}$"

$\frac{1}{2}$" DIA. HINGE HOLE

SIDE

$7\frac{1}{2}$"

$5\frac{1}{2}$"   3"

$\frac{3}{4}$"

9"

$\frac{1}{2}$" DIA. HOLES

$1\frac{3}{4}$"

$1\frac{3}{4}$"

$\frac{5}{8}$"

$1\frac{7}{8}$" RADIUS

25"

UPRIGHT

$7\frac{1}{2}$"

5"

$5\frac{1}{2}$" O.C.

$\frac{1}{2}$" DIA. HOLES

22"

8"

$\frac{1}{4}$" DEEP MORTISE GROOVE

$3\frac{1}{2}$"

$\frac{3}{4}$"

$2\frac{1}{2}$"

$1\frac{1}{2}$" $1\frac{1}{2}$"

Fig. 2-69

Fig. 2-70

GLUE

GLUE

GLUE & NAIL

SIDE

BOTTOM

TEMPORARY PROPS

DRILL $\frac{1}{2}$" DIA. HOLES TO ACCEPT THE $\frac{3}{8}$" DIA. BOLTS THAT CONNECT THE UPRIGHTS TO THE DESK SIDES

MARK

$\frac{1}{2}$"

3"

Fig. 2-72

Fig. 2-73

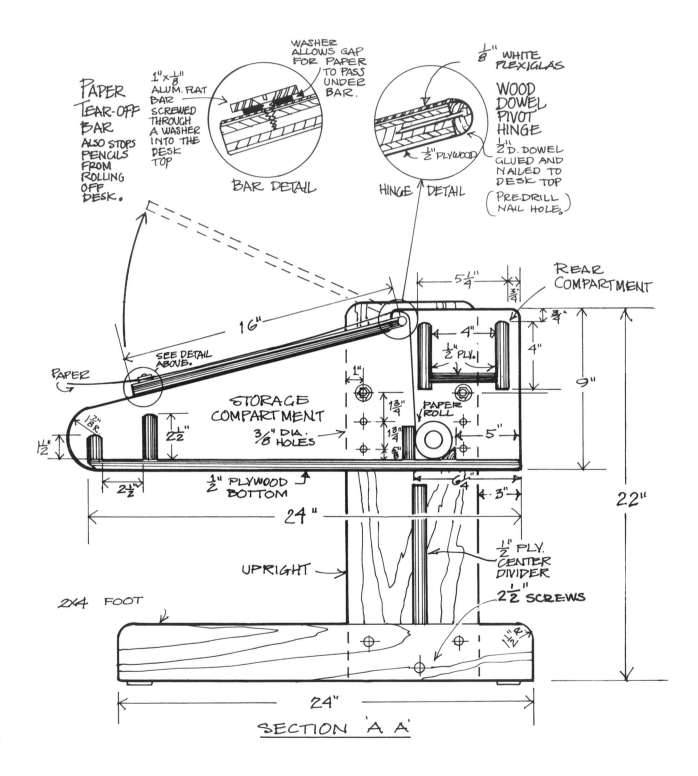

PAPER TEAR-OFF BAR ALSO STOPS PENCILS FROM ROLLING OFF DESK.

WASHER ALLOWS GAP FOR PAPER TO PASS UNDER BAR.

$1" \times \frac{1}{8}"$ ALUM. FLAT BAR SCREWED THROUGH A WASHER INTO THE DESK TOP

BAR DETAIL

$\frac{1}{8}"$ WHITE PLEXIGLAS

WOOD DOWEL PIVOT HINGE

$\frac{1}{2}"$ PLYWOOD

HINGE DETAIL

$\frac{1}{2}"$D. DOWEL GLUED AND NAILED TO DESK TOP

(PREDRILL NAIL HOLE.)

PAPER

SEE DETAIL ABOVE.

REAR COMPARTMENT

$5\frac{1}{4}"$

$\frac{3}{4}"$

$\frac{3}{4}"$

$4"$

$\frac{1}{2}"$ PLY.

$4"$

$9"$

16"

STORAGE COMPARTMENT

$\frac{3}{8}"$ DIA. HOLES

$1"$

$1\frac{3}{4}"$

$1\frac{3}{4}"$

$\frac{5}{8}"$

PAPER ROLL

$5"$

$\frac{1}{8}"$ R.

$2\frac{1}{2}"$

$\frac{1}{2}"$

$2\frac{1}{2}"$

$\frac{1}{2}"$ PLYWOOD BOTTOM

$24"$

$6\frac{1}{4}"$

$3"$

$22"$

UPRIGHT

$\frac{1}{2}"$ PLY. CENTER DIVIDER

$2\frac{1}{2}"$ SCREWS

$\frac{1}{2}"$ R.

2X4 FOOT

24"

SECTION 'A A'

Fig. 2-74

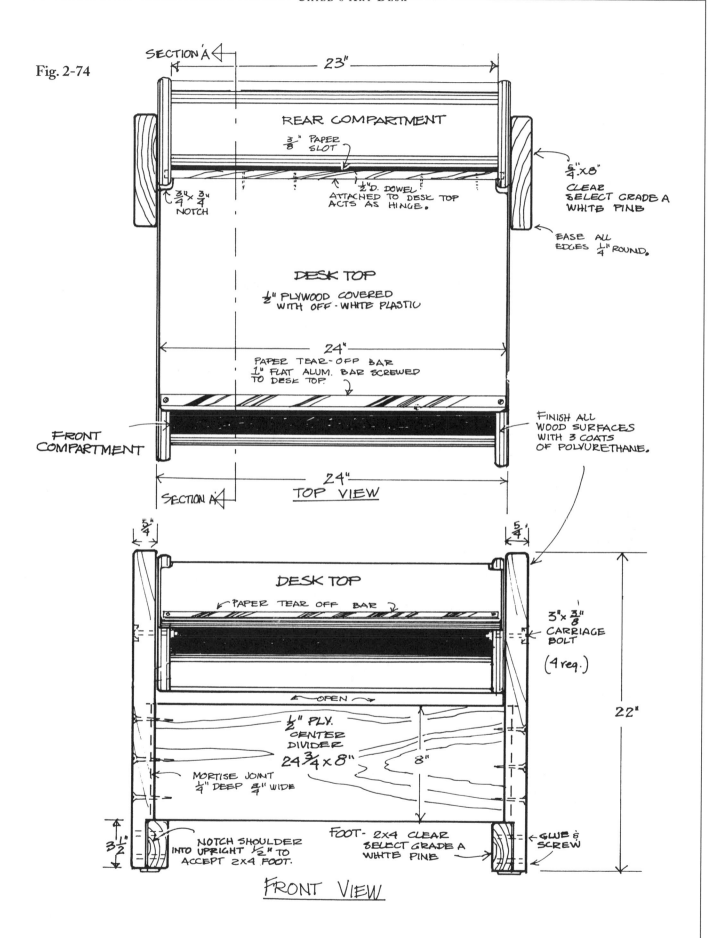

SECTION 'A'

23"

REAR COMPARTMENT

3/8" PAPER SLOT

1/2"D. DOWEL ATTACHED TO DESK TOP ACTS AS HINGE.

5/4"X8" CLEAR SELECT GRADE A WHITE PINE

3/4" X 3/4" NOTCH

EASE ALL EDGES 1/4" ROUND.

DESK TOP

1/2" PLYWOOD COVERED WITH OFF-WHITE PLASTIC

24"

PAPER TEAR-OFF BAR 1" FLAT ALUM. BAR SCREWED TO DESK TOP.

FRONT COMPARTMENT

FINISH ALL WOOD SURFACES WITH 3 COATS OF POLYURETHANE.

24"

SECTION 'A'

TOP VIEW

5/4"

5/4"

DESK TOP

PAPER TEAR OFF BAR

3"x 3/8" CARRIAGE BOLT

(4 req.)

OPEN

1/2" PLY. CENTER DIVIDER 24 3/4 x 8"

8"

22"

MORTISE JOINT 1/4" DEEP 3/4" WIDE

3 1/2"

NOTCH SHOULDER INTO UPRIGHT 1/2" TO ACCEPT 2x4 FOOT.

FOOT- 2x4 CLEAR SELECT GRADE A WHITE PINE

GLUE & SCREW

FRONT VIEW

head screws. Check for squareness and make sure the desk fits into the pedestal perfectly. After the pedestal glue is dry, round off all edges and sand smooth.

To protect the desk top and to make it easier to clean, predrill four pilot holes and screw the piece of white plexiglas to the top two corners of the desk top. Screw the aluminum bar to the lower edge of the desk, making sure to place a washer under each end of the bar to provide a space through which the paper can slide (see detail in Fig. 2-73).

To join the desk to the pedestal, carefully mark and drill a pair of ½-inch-diameter bolt holes 5 inches down from the top of each upright and 5½ inches apart (see Fig. 2-66). Lay the pedestal on its side. Position the desk between the two uprights so they extend ½ inch above the top of the desk sides and so that the back of the desk extends 3 inches beyond the sides of the uprights. Mark a line with a pencil where the pedestal intersects each side (see

Fig. 2-72). Place the drill in one of the ½-inch bolt holes and drill all the way through the side of the desk; it is important to keep the pedestal from moving. Do the same through the second hole.

To make the desk adjustable for different heights, position the desk 1¾ inches higher on the uprights and drill a second set of holes into and through the desk. Repeat this procedure a third time 1¾ inches higher. Do the same for the other side of the desk. These holes will enable the desk to grow with your child. Bolt the uprights to the desk on both sides with two ⅜-inch by 3-inch carriage bolts. Add the glide tacks to the feet.

Apply three coats of enamel paint or polyurethane to all of the bare surfaces or use polyurethane on some of the surfaces and enamel paint on others. After the desk is completely dry, insert the roll of white paper and fill the compartments with your child's art supplies.

KITCHEN CENTER AND WORKBENCH

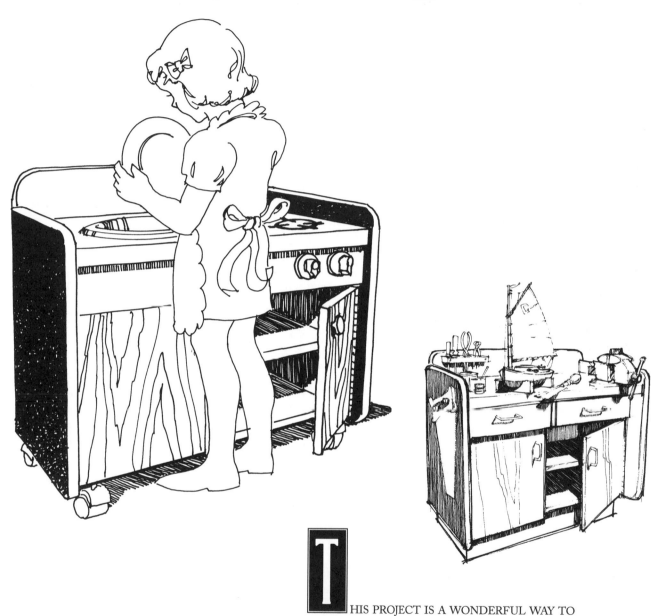

THIS PROJECT IS A WONDERFUL WAY TO provide many hours of constructive play. If your child enjoys domestic activities, this project can be made into a piece of kitchen equipment on casters that can be rolled from room to room, enabling you to keep an eye on your child while you get your own work done. Camping stores carry inexpensive sets of pots, pans, dishes and utensils. The burners for the "range," the knobs and the clock can all be designed by you and your child.

As your child grows, the kitchen center can easily be converted into a workbench. Our daughter spent hours designing and building at her workbench and derived much satisfaction from creating and constructing projects of her own.

MATERIALS FOR KITCHEN CENTER

Quantity	Size	Description	Location
2	17 inches by 24 inches	¾-inch birch veneer plywood	sides
1	17½ inches by 31 inches	¾-inch birch veneer plywood	countertop
1	12 inches by 31 inches	¾-inch birch veneer plywood	shelf
1	4 inches by 31 inches	¾-inch birch veneer plywood	control panel
1	16½ inches by 31 inches	¾-inch birch veneer plywood	bottom
2	16½ inches by 15½ inches	¾-inch birch veneer plywood	doors
1	31 inches	1x2 #2 pine	front counter support
1	5 inches by 32½ inches	¾-inch birch veneer plywood	backsplash
1	32½ inches by 27 inches	¼-inch masonite hardboard	back
4	4 inches	1x2 #2 pine	caster blocks
2	16½ inches	¾-inch by ¾-inch piano hinges and screws	
2	1⅜ inch	wood door knobs	
2	2 inch	#8 flathead screws	
1 box	1 inch	brads	
1 box	1-½ inch	finishing nails	
1 box	2 inch	finishing nails	
4	2 inch	casters (stem type)	
1 pint		polyurethane or enamel paint	
1	15-inch dia.	11-quart plastic dishpan sink	

OPTIONAL MATERIALS

Quantity	Size	Description	Location
1	⅛ inch	3½-inch dia. clear plastic	clock face
1	⅛ inch	3½-inch dia. white plastic	clock face
1	1-inch long	1-inch dia. wood dowel	timer knob
1	1¾-inch long	½-inch dia. wood dowel	timer knob
1 set	½-inch high	press-on transfer numbers	clock face
1 roll		clear tape	
1	½ inch	#6 roundhead screw and a washer	
2	1½ inch by ½ inch by ⅛ inch	wood scraps	pointer

The workbench and the kitchen center share many of the same components. There are, however, three basic differences in the construction of the two projects:

1. Instead of a front panel, the workbench has two 4-inch-high drawers (see Figs. 2-83 and 2-84), which are supported in the middle by a ¾-inch plywood center divider.

2. To protect the top of the workbench from glue and paint, a piece of ¼-inch hardboard is cut and placed over the surface.

3. A base made from 1x3 lumber is used to support the workbench rather than the four casters used in the kitchen center.

Referring to the cutting plan, (see Fig. 2-75), cut out all the pieces. Round off the top and bottom corners of the side pieces, the top corners of the masonite back panel and the edges of the side pieces. Sand the edges smooth. Cut a 2-inch by ¾-inch notch out of the top back corner of each side piece (see Fig. 2-76).

Fig. 2-75

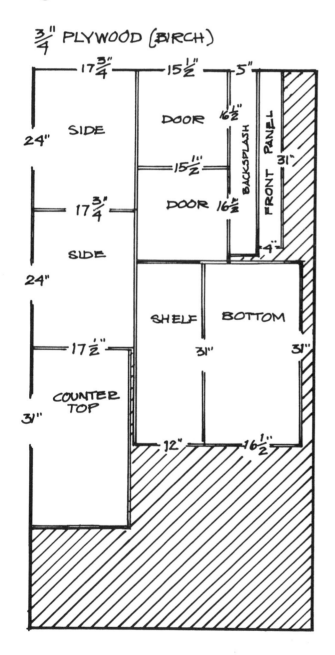

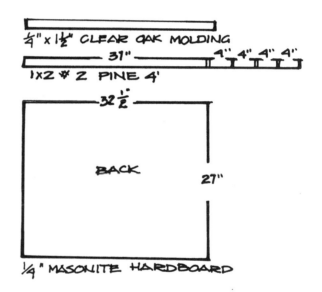

CUTTING PLAN

Trace a 14-inch diameter hole onto the plywood countertop to hold the "sink," which allows for a ½-inch overhang for the dishpan lip. If you cannot find a round dishpan of the type and size specified here, use a rectangular sink and draw the opening on the countertop based on its dimensions. Use an electric jig saw to cut out the opening for the dishpan.

Lay one of the side pieces on the floor face down,

and glue and nail (using 1½-inch finishing nails) the masonite back panel to the rear edge of the side. Stand the countertop on edge and glue the side edge of the counter to the side piece 2 inches from the top of the side piece (see Fig. 2-77). Hold the counter in position by driving a temporary nail through the back piece and into the back edge of the counter. Follow the same procedure for the shelf and the bottom piece.

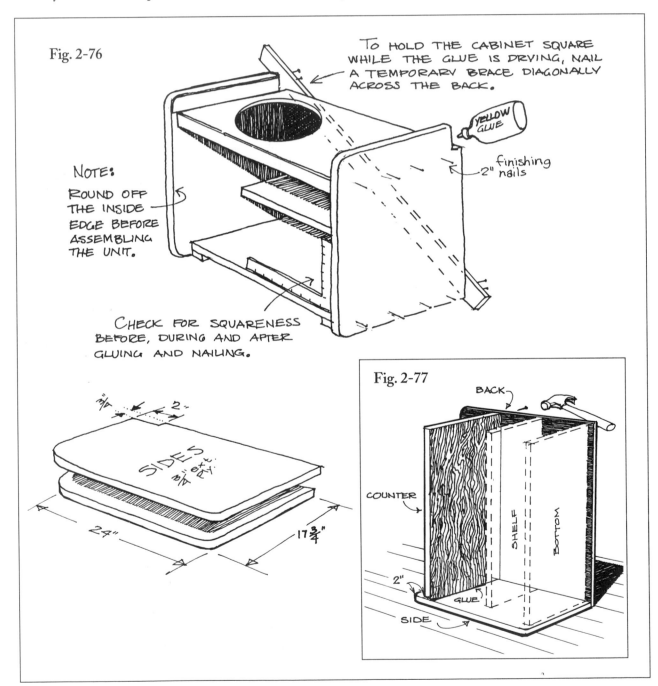

Fig. 2-76

TO HOLD THE CABINET SQUARE WHILE THE GLUE IS DRYING, NAIL A TEMPORARY BRACE DIAGONALLY ACROSS THE BACK.

YELLOW GLUE

2" finishing nails

NOTE:
ROUND OFF THE INSIDE EDGE BEFORE ASSEMBLING THE UNIT.

CHECK FOR SQUARENESS BEFORE, DURING AND AFTER GLUING AND NAILING.

¾" 2"

SIDES ¾" ext. ply.

24"

17¾"

Fig. 2-77

BACK

COUNTER

SHELF

BOTTOM

2"

GLUE

SIDE

Fig. 2-78

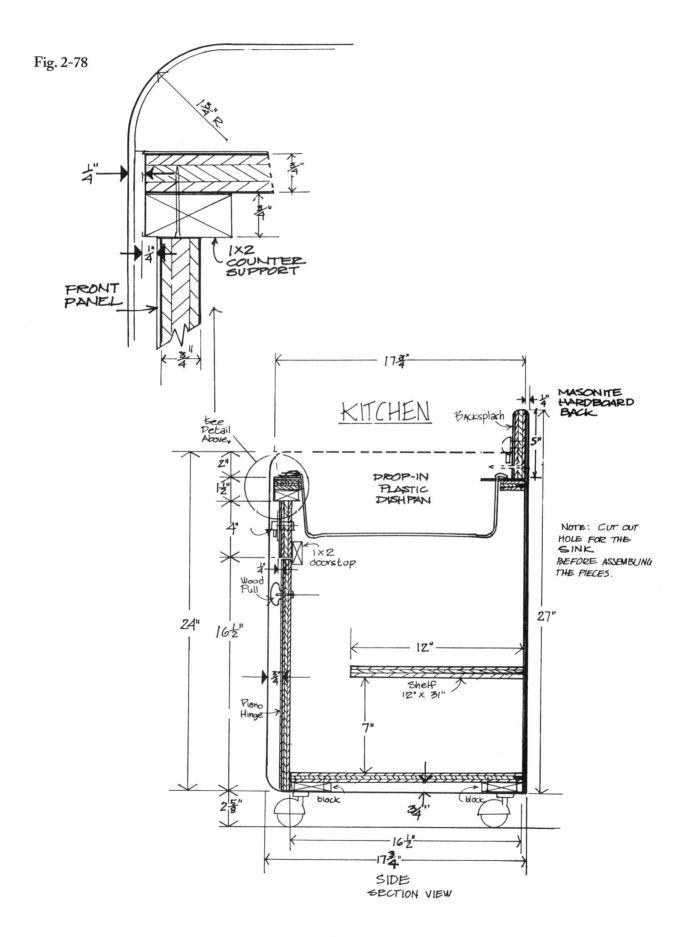

$1\frac{3}{4}$" R.

$\frac{1}{4}$"

$\frac{3}{4}$"

$\frac{3}{4}$"

$\frac{1}{4}$"

1×2
COUNTER
SUPPORT

FRONT
PANEL

$\frac{3}{4}$"

KITCHEN

$17\frac{3}{4}$"

Backsplach

MASONITE
HARDBOARD
BACK

$\frac{1}{4}$"

See
Detail
Above.

DROP-IN
PLASTIC
DISH PAN

5"

2"

$1\frac{1}{2}$"

NOTE: CUT OUT
HOLE FOR THE
SINK
BEFORE ASSEMBLING
THE PIECES.

4"

1×2
doorstop

$\frac{1}{4}$"

Wood
Pull

27"

12"

24"

$16\frac{1}{2}$"

$\frac{3}{4}$"

Shelf
12" × 31"

Piano
Hinge

7"

$2\frac{5}{8}$"

block

block

$\frac{3}{4}$"

$16\frac{1}{2}$"

$17\frac{3}{4}$"

SIDE
SECTION VIEW

Fig. 2-79

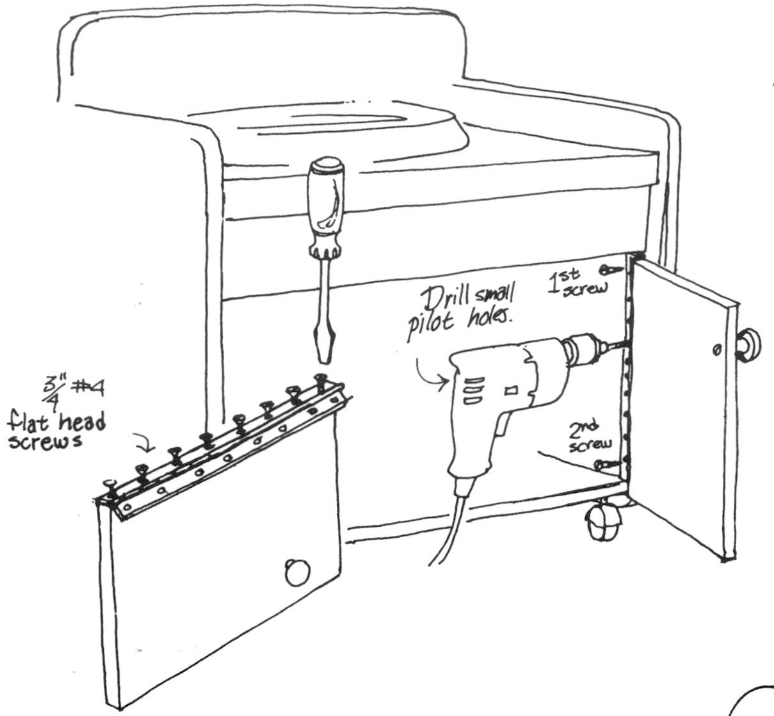

ATTACHING THE DOORS

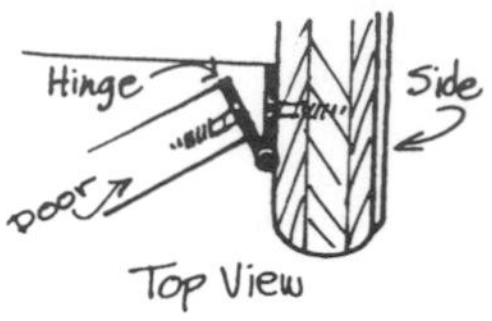

Hinge — Side

Door

Top View

TO ATTACH THE DOORS, CUT TWO PIECES OF PIANO HINGE $16\frac{1}{2}$" LONG. SCREW ALL THE SCREWS INTO THE DOOR FIRST.

MOUNT THE DOOR TO THE INSIDE WALL OF THE CABINET BY STARTING ONE SCREW AT THE TOP FIRST, AND THEN ONE AT THE BOTTOM. CHECK THE ALIGNMENT BEFORE PROCEEDING ANY FURTHER.

IT IS SIMPLER AND FASTER TO DRILL A PILOT HOLE SLIGHTLY SMALLER THAN THE SCREW ITSELF, BEFORE ATTEMPTING TO PUT THE SCREW IN.

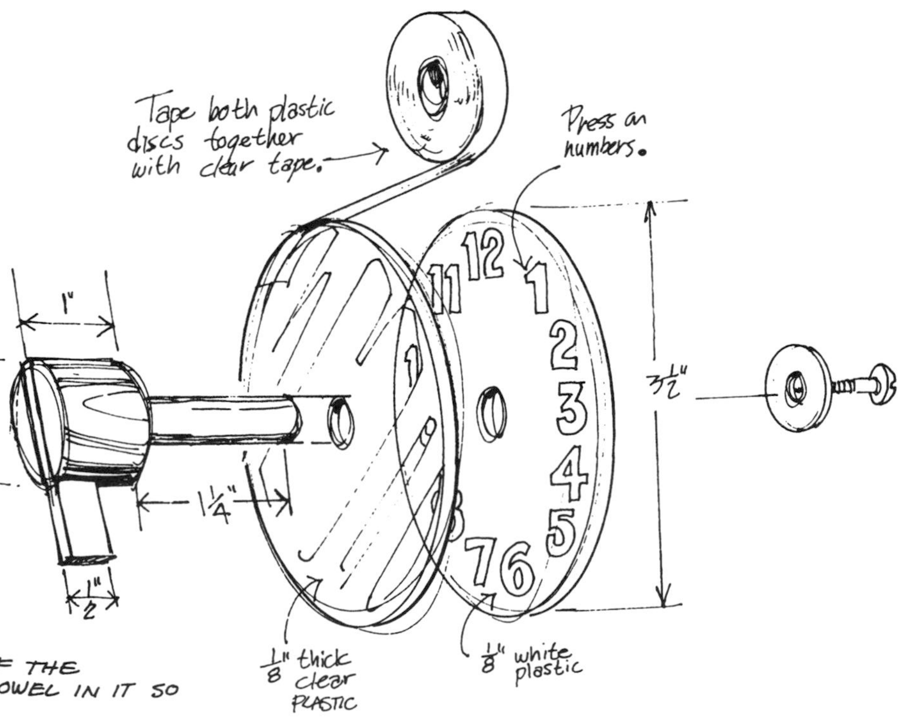

Drill small pilot holes.

1st screw

2nd screw

$\frac{3}{4}$" #4 flat head screws

Tape both plastic discs together with clear tape.

Press on numbers.

$3\frac{1}{2}$"

1"

1"

$1\frac{1}{4}$"

$\frac{1}{2}$"

$\frac{1}{8}$" thick clear plastic

$\frac{1}{8}$" white plastic

MAKE A CUT IN THE END OF A 1" DOWEL AND FIT A SMALL FLAT PIECE OF WOOD (FOR THE POINTER) IN THE SLOT. BORE A $\frac{1}{2}$" HOLE IN THE OTHER END OF THE DOWEL AND INSERT A $\frac{1}{2}$" DOWEL IN IT SO IT PROTRUDES $1\frac{1}{4}$".

CUT TWO DISCS FROM $\frac{1}{8}$" THICK PLASTIC (AS SHOWN), ADD NUMBERS AND DRILL A $\frac{1}{2}$" HOLE IN THE CENTER. DRILL AN IDENTICAL $\frac{1}{2}$" DIA. HOLE IN THE BACKSPLASH AND PUSH THE ASSEMBLY TOGETHER.

Fig. 2-80

Fig. 2-81

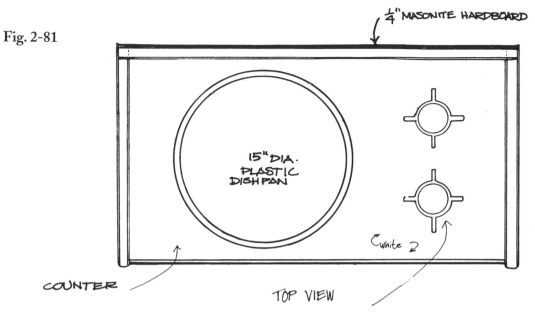

¼" MASONITE HARDBOARD

15" DIA. PLASTIC DISHPAN

Cwhite2

COUNTER

TOP VIEW

BURNERS ARE MADE BY CUTTING A MASK OUT OF
CONTACT PAPER, PRESSING IT ONTO THE COUNTER
SURFACE, AND SPRAYING IT WITH ENAMEL.
FOR A MORE PERMANENT JOB, CUT A ⅛" DEEP
GROOVE WITH A ROUTER AND FILL THE RECESS
WITH GREY EPOXY PASTE.

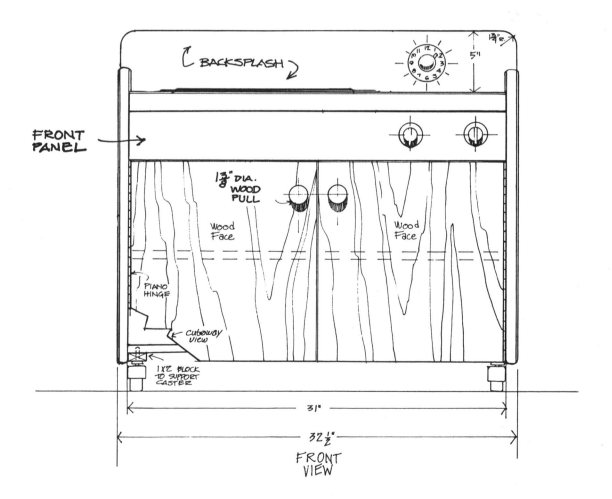

BACKSPLASH

1¾"R.

5"

FRONT PANEL

1⅜" DIA. WOOD PULL

Wood Face

Wood Face

PIANO HINGE

Cutaway View

1x2 BLOCK TO SUPPORT CASTER

31"

32½"

FRONT VIEW

Carefully lay the other side over the exposed ends of the counter, shelf and bottom pieces, and — after making sure that they are properly aligned and everything is perfectly square — glue and nail the remaining side to the counter, shelf and bottom pieces. Note that to ensure that the unit remains perfectly square so that the doors will fit later on, nail a temporary diagonal brace (made from scrap lumber) across the back. This brace holds the pieces squarely in position while the glue is drying (see Fig. 2-76). After the glue has dried, turn the unit over onto its other side and nail this side to the other ends of the counter, shelf and bottom. Check again for squareness. It is essential that the assembly be perfectly square.

The backsplash rests on the countertop, fitting into the notched-out area of the sides. Using several clamps, glue the back of the backsplash to the masonite back panel and the countertop. Drive #8 2-inch flathead screws through the back panel top corners, through the backsplash and into the notched edge of the side panels. Glue and nail the 31-inch-long 1x2 underneath the front of the counter (see Fig. 2-78).

After the glue dries, glue the top edge of the 4-inch by 31-inch front panel to the lower side of the front of the counter support and nail through the side pieces and into the side edges of the front panel. Using 1½-inch finishing nails, glue and nail a 1x2 to the back of the front panel so that it extends ½ inch below the bottom of the front panel and acts as a stop for the door (see Fig. 2-78).

Attach one side of each piano hinge to the doors (see Fig. 2-79) and then attach the other side of the hinge to the inside of the kitchen unit. Fasten the bottom and top screws, check for door alignment, adjust and drive in the remaining screws. Note that it is simpler and faster to drill a pilot hole slightly smaller than the screw before driving in the screws. Install one 1⅜-inch diameter doorknob on each door (see Fig. 2-81). Finish with polyurethane or enamel paint.

To hold the four casters, glue and then nail the four 4-inch-long 1x2s to the inside corners of the kitchen bottom using 1½-inch finishing nails. Drill holes in the blocks to accept the casters.

Lay the plastic dishpan into the opening in the countertop. Sterilite makes an inexpensive heavy-duty plastic dishpan or buy a rectangular version from any discount or hardware store.

The timer clock and burners are purely for decoration and can be made according to the specifications in Figs. 2-80 and 2-81, or you can purchase at most hardware or building supply stores inexpensive wooden knobs or plastic replacement knobs for a gas range.

WORKBENCH

To build the workbench, follow the same steps for the kitchen center up to the point where casters are added and omit the earlier procedure for the front panel. Instead of the front panel, fill the 4-inch space under the top with two tool drawers. Make a center divider (to hold the drawers in place) from a ¾-inch by 4¾-inch by 17¼-inch piece of plywood and mount it underneath the center of the countertop using four #10 2-inch flathead screws spaced equidistantly (see Fig. 2-84). Take the piece of oak molding and glue it to the front edge of the plywood bench top and the 1x2 support piece (see Fig. 2-83).

Referring to pages 29-31 and Fig. 2-84, construct two drawers 15 inches wide and 17 inches

MATERIALS FOR WORKBENCH

Quantity	Size	Description	Location
2	17¾ inches by 24 inches	¾-inch birch veneer plywood	sides
1	17½ inches by 31 inches	¾-inch birch veneer plywood	workbench top
1	16½ inches by 31 inches	¼-inch masonite hardboard	protective surface
1	12 inches by 31 inches	¾-inch birch veneer plywood	shelf
1	4¾ inches by 17¼ inches	¾-inch birch veneer plywood	center divider
1	31 inches	¼-inch by 1½-inch clear oak molding	front edge
2	15 inches by 4 inches	¾-inch birch veneer plywood	drawer faces
4	16¼ inches	1x4 clear pine	drawer sides
2	13½ inches	1x4 clear pine	drawer fronts
2	14 inches	1x4 clear pine	drawer backs
2	15¼ inches by 14 inches	¼-inch masonite hardboard	drawer bottoms
4	16½ inches	¼-inch by ¾-inch clear pine	drawer cleats
1	16½ inches by 31 inches	¾-inch plywood	bottom
2	16½ inches by 15½ inches	¾-inch plywood	doors
1	31 inches	1x2 #2 pine	front counter support
1	31 inches	1x2 #2 pine	door stop
4	4 inches	1x2 #2 pine	caster blocks
1	5 inches by 32½ inches	¾-inch birch veneer plywood	backsplash
1	32½ inches by 27 inches	¼-inch masonite hardboard	back
2	31 inches	1x3 #2 pine	base
2	12¾ inches	1x3 #2 pine	base
2	16½ inches	¾-inch by ¾-inch piano hinges and screws	
2	3 inches	wire pull handles	drawers
8	2 inch	#8 flathead screws	back panel
1 box	1 inch	brads	
1 box	1½ inch	finishing nails	
1 box	2 inch	finishing nails	
1 pint		polyurethane or enamel paint	

deep. Make the drawer faces from the ¾-inch by 15-inch by 4-inch pieces of plywood, the sides from the 16¼-inch-long 1x4s, the backs from 14-inch-long 1x4s and the false fronts from 13½-inch-long 1x4s.

Cut the 15¼-inch-deep by 14-inch-wide bottom of the drawer from the masonite. The drawers ride on ¼-inch by ¾-inch cleats, screwed to the sides of

the workbench. Cut ¼-inch by $^{13}/_{16}$-inch grooves on the outside of each drawer ¾ inch up from the bottom of the drawer sides. Measure and mark where the cleats will be screwed to the sides of the workbench (see Fig. 2-84).

To give the workbench a solid foundation, build a base out of the four pieces of #2 pine 1x3. Glue the front and back pieces to the ends of the side pieces to form a rectangle, fastening with 2-inch finishing nails. Place this base unit under the workbench (see Fig. 2-83). Glue and nail the workbench to the base by nailing through the bottom of the workbench into the tops of the 1x3 pieces.

Lay the piece of masonite over the plywood top of the workbench. This removable top protects the underlying plywood surface. You can build a simple tool rack for small tools by boring various-sized holes in a scrap 2x4 block. Screw the rack onto the backsplash from the back side of the wood. Larger tools will fit into the two drawers underneath and saws will rest easily on wooden dowels placed on the side of the workbench out of harm's way.

Fig. 2-82

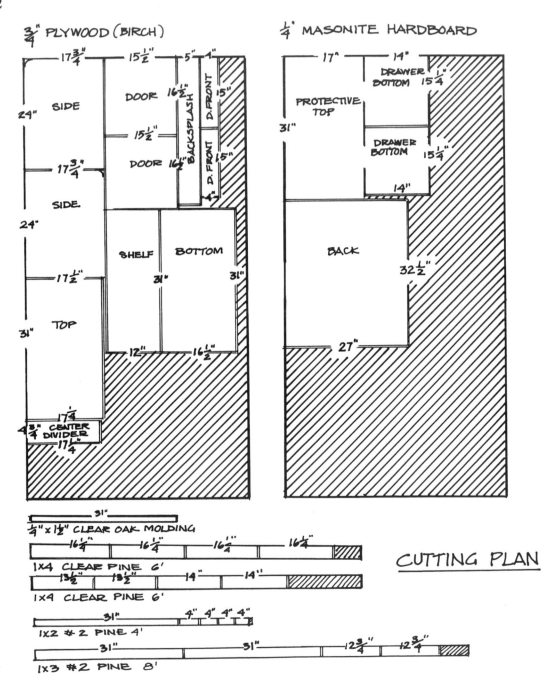

CUTTING PLAN

Fig. 2-83

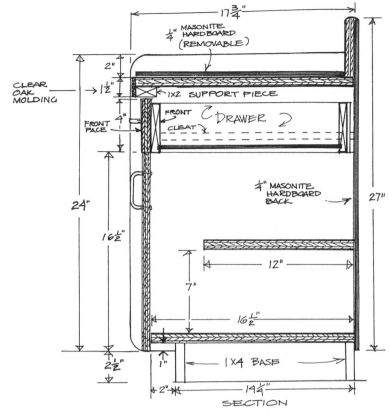

17¾"

¼" MASONITE HARDBOARD (REMOVABLE)

2"

1½"

CLEAR OAK MOLDING

1x2 SUPPORT PIECE

FRONT FACE

FRONT CLEAT

4"

DRAWER 2

¼" MASONITE HARDBOARD BACK

27"

24"

16½"

12"

7"

16½"

1"

1x4 BASE

2½"

2"

14¼"

SECTION

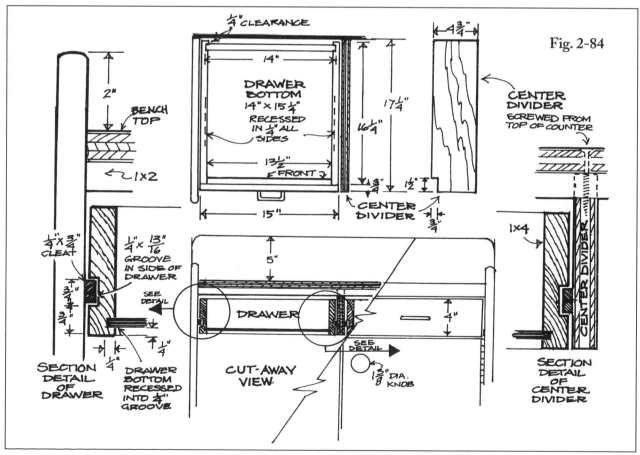

¼" CLEARANCE

14"

DRAWER BOTTOM 14" x 15¼" RECESSED IN ¼" ALL SIDES

13½"

FRONT

15"

17¼"

16¼"

4¾"

1½"

¾"

CENTER DIVIDER

¾"

4¾"

CENTER DIVIDER SCREWED FROM TOP OF COUNTER

Fig. 2-84

2"

BENCH TOP

1x2

¼" x ¾" CLEAT

1" x 13/16" GROOVE IN SIDE OF DRAWER

SEE DETAIL

¾"

¾"

¼"

¼"

SECTION DETAIL OF DRAWER

DRAWER BOTTOM RECESSED INTO ¼" GROOVE

5"

DRAWER

CUT-AWAY VIEW

SEE DETAIL

4"

1⅜" DIA. KNOB

1x4

CENTER DIVIDER

SECTION DETAIL OF CENTER DIVIDER

COMPUTER CENTER

THIS COMPUTER CENTER CAN BE constructed from two 4x8 sheets of ¾-inch melamine or plywood. We used white melamine and finished the edges with melamine edging tape.

The keyboard shelf slides in and out of slots created by two side cleats and a stationary supporting panel underneath. Be sure that the space provided allows ample room for the keyboard to slide easily. If you use plywood and finish with polyurethane, the thickness of several coats may make the shelf bind. Whatever building material you choose, we recommend attaching Nylo tape, which can be ordered from the Woodworkers' Store (see Sources). This helps the shelf to slide more smoothly. The keyboard shelf has plenty of room for a computer's mouse and miscellaneous materials. The top shelf supports the monitor and the printer. Paper for the printer can be stored on a separate shelf underneath the sliding keyboard panel. An additional shelf is provided at the bottom of the desk for manuals and reference books.

MATERIALS

Quantity	Size	Description	Location
2	4x8 sheets	¾-inch white melamine or birch veneer plywood	sides, back, shelves, middle divider, top, keyboard shelf and cleats
1	40½ inch	1x2 clear pine	face of keyboard shelf
1 roll	¾ inch	Nylo tape	cleats and keyboard shelf
1 box	1¼ inch	#8 flathead screws	
1 box	1⅝ inch	white panel nails	
1 pint		polyurethane	edge of keyboard shelf
1 roll		melamine edging tape	melamine edges
6	1 inch	nylon glide tacks	

Fig. 2-85

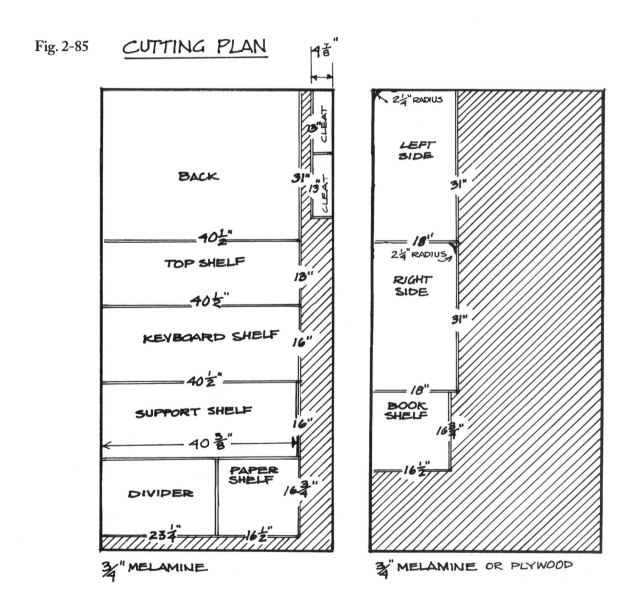

CUTTING PLAN

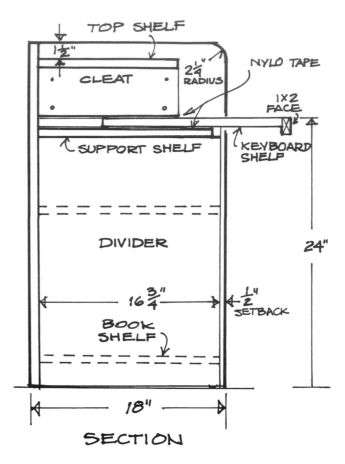

egin by cutting out all the pieces as shown on the cutting plan (see Fig. 2-85). You will have more than half a sheet of plywood or melamine left over, so set this aside for another project. Lay both side pieces on the floor with the good faces down. Glue and then screw (#8 1¼-inch screws) the cleats to the interior faces of the two side pieces ¾ inch from the rear edge of the side and 2¼ inches down from the top edge of the side (see Fig. 2-86).

Stand the side pieces on edge and have another person help you hold them in position while you rest the back on the side cleats. Glue and nail the sides to the back. If you are using melamine, drill pilot holes before hammering in the nails (see Fig. 1-12, page 23 for instructions on nailing melamine).

Stand the unit right side up and lay the top shelf on the cleats and against the back of the unit. Glue and nail the top shelf in place, hammering nails every 2 inches through the back of the desk unit into the rear edge of the top shelf.

Glue and nail the support shelf ⅞ inch below the bottom of the cleats, allowing clearance for the ¾-inch-wide keyboard shelf to slide in and out (see Fig. 2-87). Glue and nail the piece of 1x2 clear pine facing to the front edge of the keyboard shelf. Attach Nylo tape to the bottom edge of the cleats and underneath the keyboard panel where the two pieces are in contact. This creates a smooth surface on which the shelf can slide.

Next, attach the middle divider to the two side shelves (the book and paper shelves). To do this, glue and nail one side of the lower shelf to the divider 2 inches from the bottom of the divider. Then glue and nail the upper shelf to the divider 6 inches from the top of the divider. Attach the divider and the shelves to the desk unit by hammering 1⅝-inch nails through the back of the desk unit into the rear edge of the divider every 2 inches. Attach the other sides of the shelves by nailing 1⅝-inch finishing

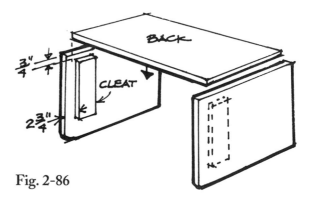

Fig. 2-86

nails every 2 inches through the side of the desk into the ends of the shelves after checking to make sure the shelves are level before hammering the nails all the way in (see note above on hammering if using melamine instead of plywood).

Note that you should test the keyboard shelf by sliding it into the slot provided by the cleats and the support shelf. If it sticks, spray it with a silicone

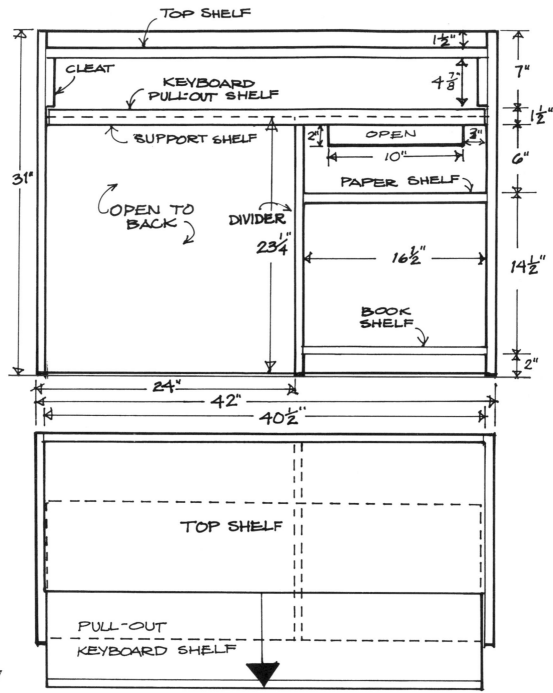

Fig. 2-87

spray. If you are using melamine board, cover the edges with melamine edging tape (see Fig. 1-11, page 23). Cover the nail holes with white spackle and sand lightly. Sand the front facing of the pull-out shelf until smooth and cover with three coats of polyurethane. If you are using plywood for the rest of the pieces, also paint the remaining visible surfaces with three coats of polyurethane.

Apply six nylon glide tacks to the bottom edges of the desk to prevent the unit from scratching the floor.

STORAGE

TOY STORAGE UNIT

THE TOY STORAGE UNIT WE BUILT has had a long and useful life. Originally, it was used to store our two-year-old's dolls, costumes, pull toys and — at times — out-of-season clothes. As our daughter grew older, she filled it with larger toys and sporting equipment. When she entered high school, we converted it into a filing cabinet, which is what it still functions as today. This is a simple design and should take you no more than one weekend to build.

MATERIALS

Quantity	Size	Description	Location
1	4x8 sheet	¾-inch birch veneer plywood	sides, back, drawer faces, bottom and top
1	4x4 sheet	¼-inch masonite hardboard	drawer bottoms
1	4x8 sheet	½-inch birch veneer plywood	drawer sides, backs and fronts
1	17½ inches	¼-inch by 2-inch clear oak molding	
4	2 inch dia.	casters (stem type)	
2 pairs	18 inch	telescoping drawer slides and screws	
2	4 inches	1-inch dia. wood dowel	drawer pull
2	3 inches wide and long	⅛-inch-thick leather strap	drawer pull
1 box	1½ inch	finishing nails	
1 quart		polyurethane or enamel paint	

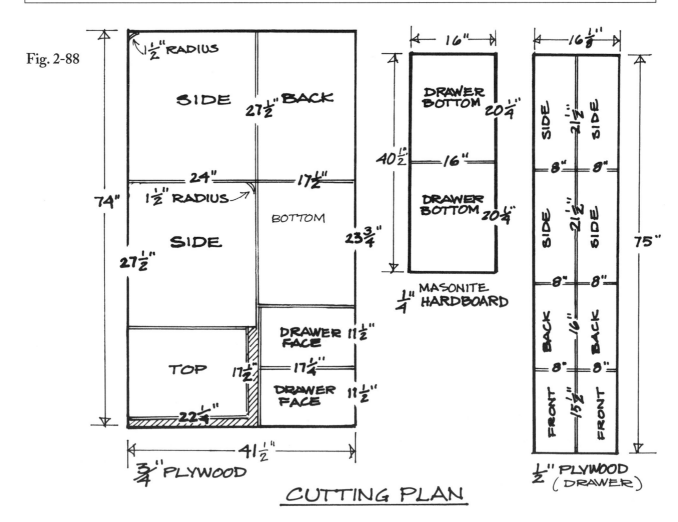

Fig. 2-88

CUTTING PLAN

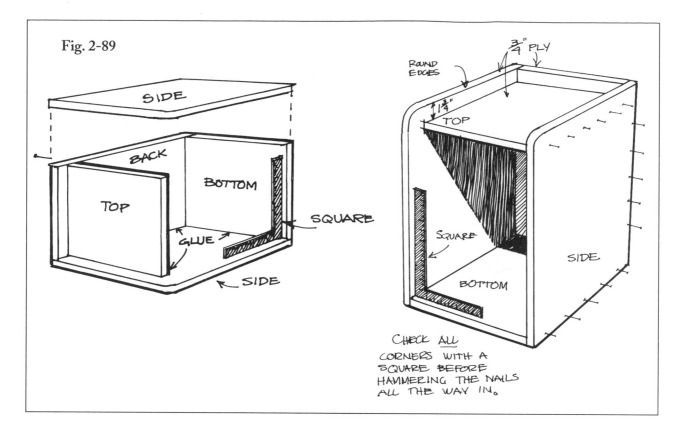

Fig. 2-89

eferring to the cutting plan (see Fig. 2-88), cut out all the pieces. Draw a 1½-inch radius on the two top corners of the side pieces, round them off with a router or file (see page 26) and sand smooth.

Lay one side piece on the floor with the good face down, making sure that the rounded corner is in the correct position (see Fig. 2-89). Glue the back and bottom pieces to the side piece. Note that the bottom piece is placed inside the back and side pieces so that the end grain will not show and the back piece is placed inside the side piece.

Measure and mark a line 1¾ inches from the top of the back and side pieces. Place the top surface of the top piece flush with the line, then glue it to the back and side pieces. Measure 1¾ inches from the top of the second side piece, apply glue to the exposed top edges of the unit and carefully lay the second side piece in place. Before nailing the unit together, you must make sure the sides are square

with the bottom and top since this affects how the drawers will fit (see Fig. 2-90).

Mark a center line for the nails on the outside face, driving the nails through the sides into the edges of the back and bottom pieces. Finish the nailing by sinking the nail heads in ⅛ inch and filling the holes with wood putty.

DRAWERS

Gather together the cut pieces of masonite and ½-inch plywood for the drawers. To make the drawer joints, use an electric router or a table saw to cut a ¼-inch-wide dado that is ¼ inch deep and ¼ inch up from the bottom edge of the back piece, the two side pieces and the front of the drawer. If you don't have a tool to cut the dadoes, refer to pages 29-31 for instructions on how to build simple lap-joint drawers. There's nothing wrong with doing the drawers that way—just be sure to make adjustments in the measurements for the back and bottom.

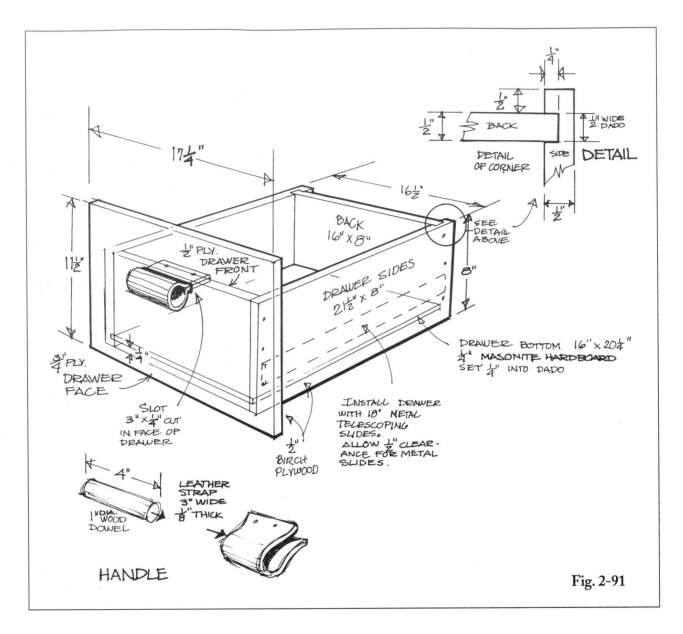

DETAIL

DETAIL OF CORNER

¼" WIDE DADO

BACK

SIDE

17¼"

16½"

BACK
16" x 8"

11½"

½" PLY.
DRAWER
FRONT

DRAWER SIDES
2½" x 8"

8"

SEE DETAIL ABOVE

¾" PLY.
DRAWER
FACE

SLOT
3" x ¼" CUT
IN FACE OF
DRAWER

½"
BIRCH
PLYWOOD

INSTALL DRAWER
WITH 18" METAL
TELESCOPING
SLIDES.
ALLOW ½" CLEAR-
ANCE FOR METAL
SLIDES.

DRAWER BOTTOM 16" x 20¼"
¼" MASONITE HARDBOARD
SET ¼" INTO DADO

4"

1" DIA.
WOOD
DOWEL

LEATHER
STRAP
3" WIDE
⅛" THICK

HANDLE

Fig. 2-91

On the interior of the two side pieces, make a ¼-inch-deep dado ½ inch wide and ½ inch from the back end to accept the back piece (see detail in Fig. 2-91). Glue and insert the back piece into these ½-inch-wide grooves. Slide the masonite drawer bottom into the ¼-inch grooves of the sides and back.

Place the drawer front between the two sides while fitting the masonite drawer bottom into the ¼-inch groove of the drawer front. Glue and nail the two sides to the drawer front using the 1½-inch finishing nails. Repeat these steps for the second drawer.

After making sure both drawers are square, glue and clamp the drawer faces onto the fronts of the drawers. Position each drawer face so that the bottom of the face is flush with the drawer bottom and the drawer face overlaps the sides of the drawer by ½ inch on both sides.

The drawer handle can be made any way you wish. For the one pictured here, use an electric jig saw to cut a ¼-inch by 3-inch slot out of the drawer face on both drawers. The slot should be positioned just above the drawer front.

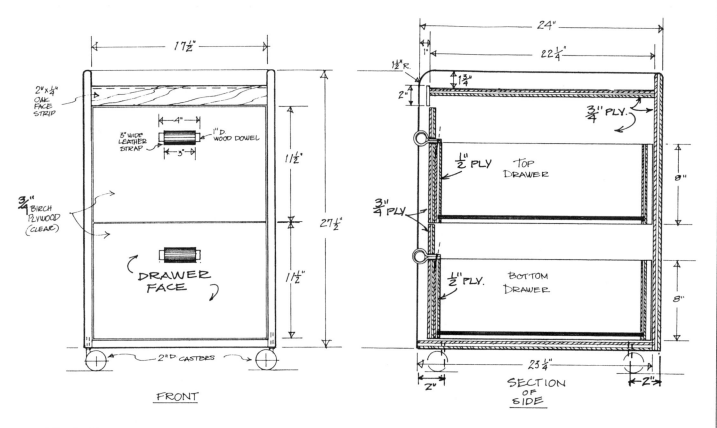

Fig. 2-92

Fig. 2-93

Fold the leather strap in half and around the wooden dowel and insert the ends of the strap through the slot. Secure the ends on the inside by nailing down through the leather into the top of the drawer front with 1½-inch finishing nails.

Since the storage drawers may hold heavy loads, it's best to hang them on 18-inch telescoping slides (see Fig. 2-94). Directions for hanging these are on the package they come in. To enable you to easily move the unit from room to room, we recommend attaching 2-inch diameter casters to the base (see Figs. 2-92 and 2-93).

Cut the piece of clear ¼-inch by 2-inch oak molding 17 inches long; glue and nail in place with 1½-inch finishing nails. Finally, give all exposed wood a final light sanding and finish with three coats of polyurethane or enamel paint.

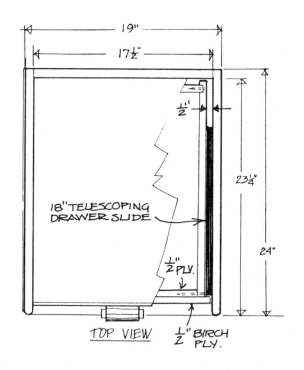

Fig. 2-94

PORTABLE STORAGE WAGON

THIS LITTLE WAGON IS APPRECIATED by adults as well as children. For a child it serves as a means of transportation and is an excellent way of discovering locomotion. For parents, it is a storage place for toys and a convenient way for teaching a child to pick up. Cleaning can actually be a happy time and a source of accomplishment for a child when introduced as a game.

After your child outgrows the storage wagon, it can still come in handy around the house. It can be used to store painting supplies or magazines or as a container for a large potted plant that can be easily rolled to a sunny location as the seasons change. If heavy-duty casters are used for wheels, very weighty objects can be moved by balancing them on top of the toy bin. Casters come in two basic shapes, plate or stem (see Fig. 2-99). The most common type available are the white nylon casters sold in most hardware stores. Whichever type you choose, make sure the casters are at least 2 inches in diameter so they will roll over rugs and door sills easily.

MATERIALS

Quantity	Size	Description	Location
1	4x4 sheet	¾-inch plywood	bottom, sides and ends
4	2¼ inches	casters (plate type)	
1	4 inches	1-inch dia. dowel	handle
1	2 feet	⅜-inch dia. rope handle	
1 box	2 inch	finishing nails	joints
1 pint		polyurethane	
1 pint		enamel paint	

Fig. 2-95

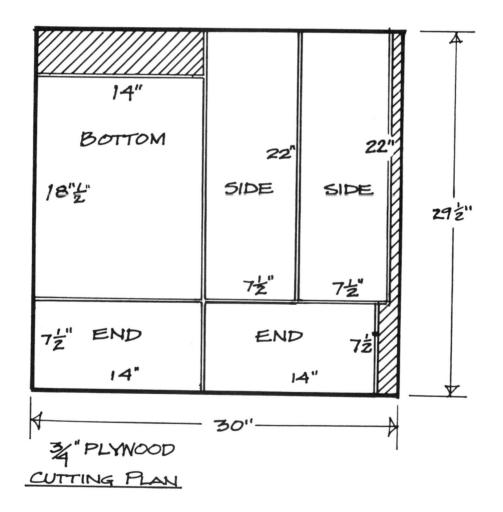

¾" PLYWOOD
CUTTING PLAN

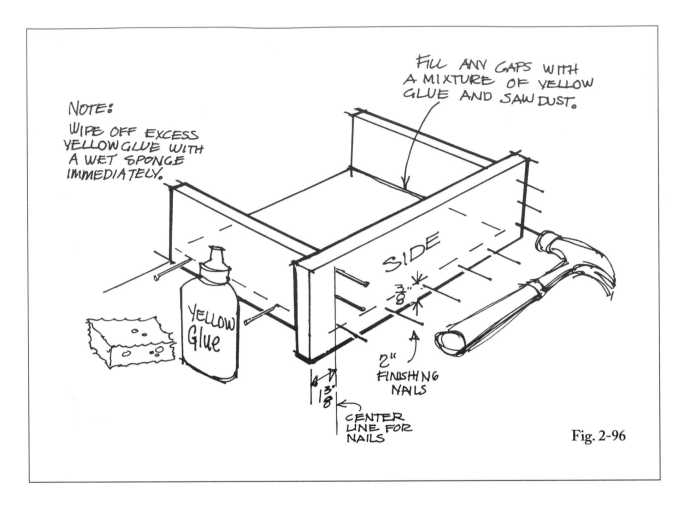

NOTE:
WIPE OFF EXCESS YELLOW GLUE WITH A WET SPONGE IMMEDIATELY.

FILL ANY GAPS WITH A MIXTURE OF YELLOW GLUE AND SAWDUST.

SIDE

YELLOW Glue

3"/8

2" FINISHING NAILS

1 3"/8

CENTER LINE FOR NAILS

Fig. 2-96

Since this is basically a box on wheels, it is one of the easiest projects in this book to make—a nice rainy-day job for dad or mom and a good project for the inexperienced. To keep it simple, we have eliminated difficult dado joints.

To begin, cut out all the pieces according to the cutting plan (see Fig. 2-95). If desired, the sides and the ends can also be cut from a 6-foot-long 1x8.

Draw a line ⅜ inch up from the bottom of the end and side pieces (see Fig. 2-96). This is where the side and end pieces will be nailed to the bottom piece. To mark where the end pieces should be positioned with regard to the side pieces, measure 1 inch from each end of the sides and draw a vertical line. Lay one of the sides on a flat surface face up and hammer three 2-inch finishing nails 1⅜ inches from the side ends so that the points are just barely

poking out through the other side.

To attach the side to the end pieces, place the two ends against a wall with the bottom piece between them. Apply glue to the edges of the end and bottom pieces and nail the side onto the two end pieces. Turn the unit around and do the same with the other side piece, making sure the bottom fits snugly.

Nail the sides and ends to the bottom piece. However, before driving the nails all the way in, check to see that everything is positioned correctly. Recess the finishing nails below the surface of the wood by hammering them down with a nail set (see Fig. 1-23, page 31). Fill the nail holes with wood putty and sand the surfaces smooth. Round off all corners and edges with a file and sandpaper.

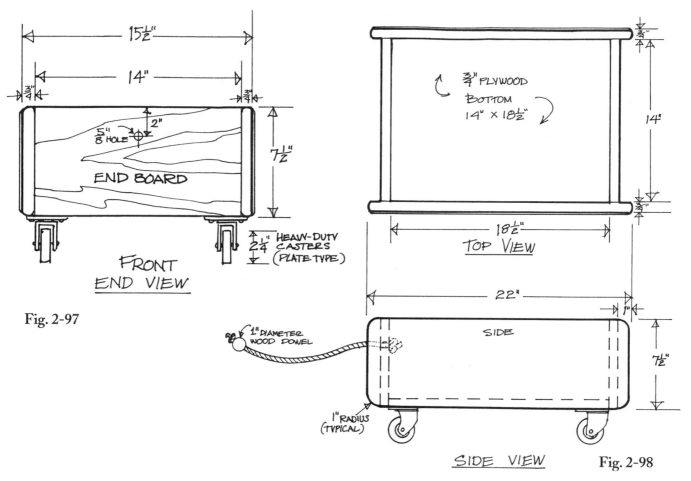

15½"

14"

¾"

⅝" HOLE

2"

END BOARD

7½"

HEAVY-DUTY CASTERS (PLATE-TYPE)
2¼"

FRONT
END VIEW

Fig. 2-97

¾" PLYWOOD
BOTTOM
14" × 18½"

¾"

14"

¾"

18½"
TOP VIEW

22"

1"

SIDE

1" DIAMETER
WOOD DOWEL

7½"

1" RADIUS
(TYPICAL)

SIDE VIEW

Fig. 2-98

CASTERS COME IN MANY SIZES AND STYLES

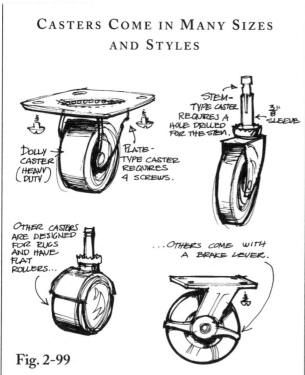

STEM-TYPE CASTER REQUIRES A HOLE DRILLED FOR THE STEM.

⅜" SLEEVE

DOLLY CASTER (HEAVY DUTY)

PLATE-TYPE CASTER REQUIRES 4 SCREWS.

OTHER CASTERS ARE DESIGNED FOR RUGS AND HAVE FLAT ROLLERS...

...OTHERS COME WITH A BRAKE LEVER.

Fig. 2-99

For the rope handle, bore a ⅝-inch-wide hole 2 inches from the top of the front end and centered end to end (see Fig. 2-97). Thread the rope through the hole and tie a stop knot at the end. Bore a hole through the center of the wooden dowel, thread the free end of the rope through the hole and tie another knot (see Fig. 2-98).

Paint the interior and exterior ends of the wagon with three coats of polyurethane. After the last coat has dried, paint the interior and exterior of the sides a bright color using enamel paint. Lastly, screw the four casters to the bottom of the wagon. Now, child and toys are ready to roll.

Audio-Video Center

OPENING THE DOOR OF A TEENAGER'S room can be a daunting experience! Although they always seem to be able to find things in spite of the mess and confusion, one way of helping them get organized is by designing and building a storage unit that consolidates all audio and video equipment. Tapes stored in a compartmentalized drawer will suffer less damage and remain dust free, and having the floor of a teenager's room visible will strengthen lines of communication between teenagers and parents. Obviously, the storage center also makes a nice storage unit for the family to share and might be useful for a family room or den, depending on your situation.

MATERIALS

Quantity	Size	Description	Location
1	4x4 sheet	¾-inch birch veneer plywood	all flat pieces but drawer bottoms and back rails
1	4x4 sheet	¼-inch masonite hardboard	drawer bottoms
2	42 inches	1x3 #2 pine	back rails
2	3 inch	wire pulls	drawer handles
4	10 inch	telescoping slides and screws	drawers
2	2 inch	molly bolts	
1 roll	¾ inch	edging tape	shelf, front edges
1 box	1½-inch	finishing nails	
1 quart		polyurethane or enamel paint	

Fig. 2-100

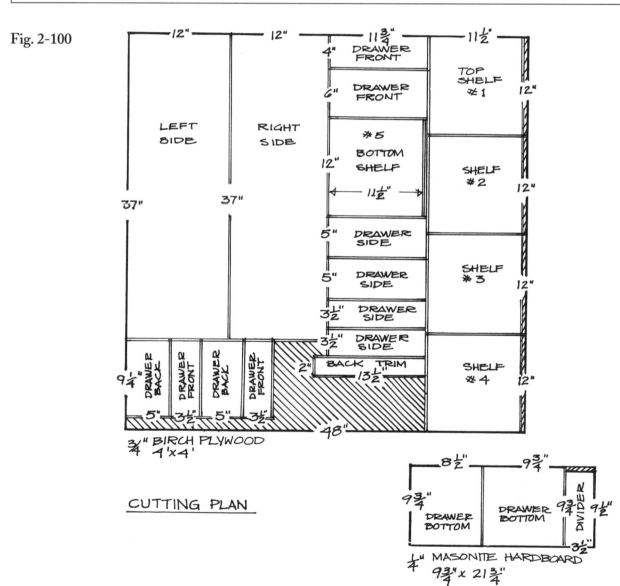

CUTTING PLAN

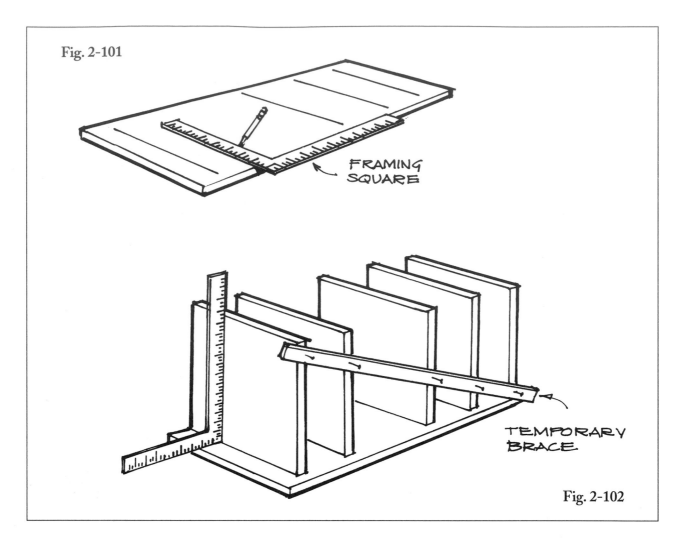

Fig. 2-101

FRAMING SQUARE

TEMPORARY BRACE

Fig. 2-102

If the dimensions we have listed do not conform to your own equipment, carefully measure what you have and make a revised cutting plan, using the one here as a guide. The dimensions for the unit below are for standard, moderately priced equipment with an average width of 11 inches.

This practical space-saving storage center is designed to hold a television, VCR, CD player, radio, amplifier, tape deck and numerous videos and audiocassettes. When your child reaches college age, it can also serve as a storage box for transporting this same equipment. Wrap the various pieces in bubble wrap or foam core, place them in the designated compartments and lay the unit on its back for traveling. The back of the unit is left open for ventilation and to allow space for the connecting wires.

This project can be cut from one piece of plywood or melamine and constructed in only a day.

Cut out all the pieces, as shown in the cutting plan (see Fig. 2-100). Using a framing square and pencil, mark on the inside surfaces of the two side pieces where the top edge of each shelf will go (see Fig. 2-101). On the outside of each side piece, use a framing square and pencil to locate the center line of each shelf and make a light dashed line to indicate where the nails should go.

Lay one of the side pieces on the floor face down (make sure there are no nails or other sharp objects on the floor that could mar the surface of the plywood). One by one, glue the shelves into position, checking as you go to make sure that they are

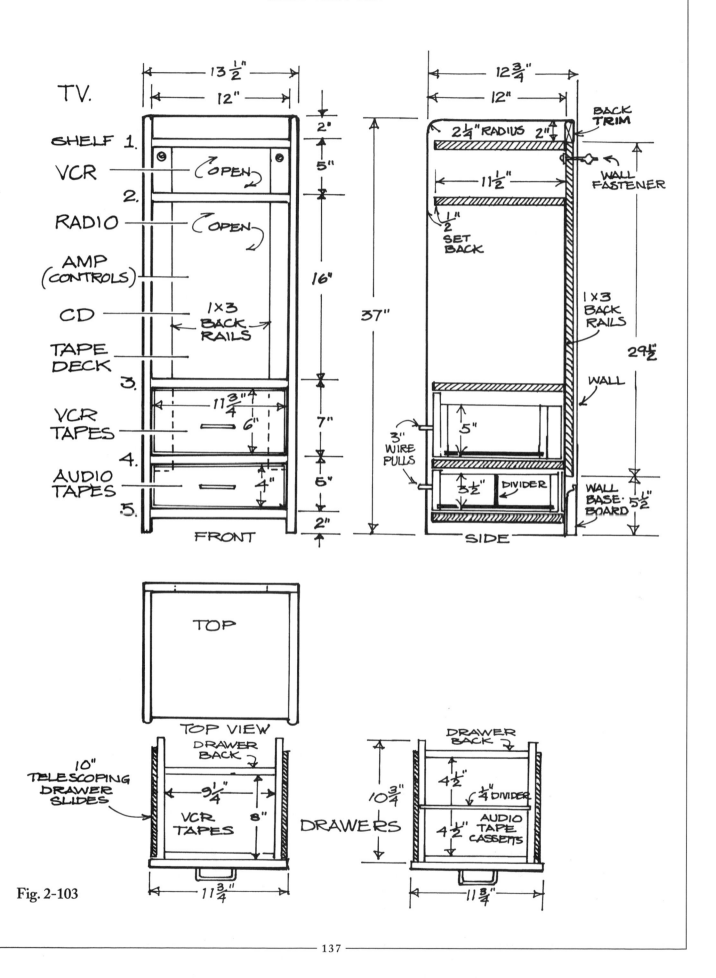

Fig. 2-103

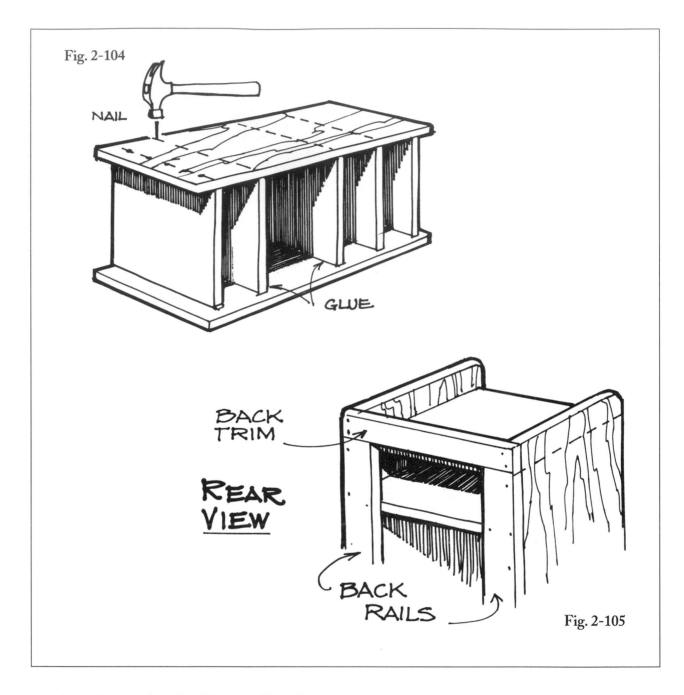

Fig. 2-104

NAIL

GLUE

BACK TRIM

REAR VIEW

BACK RAILS

Fig. 2-105

at right angles with the side of the unit. To hold the shelves in place while the glue is drying, temporarily connect them with a thin strip of wood nailed diagonally along the outside edges of the shelves (see Fig. 2-102).

Apply glue to the exposed side edges of the shelves. Lay the second side piece on the floor face down. Carefully lift up the first side with the shelves attached to it and position the exposed shelf edges

over the premarked lines on the second side piece, again checking for squareness. After the glue has dried, drive 1½-inch finishing nails through the side piece and into the edges of the shelves every 2 inches (see Fig. 2-104). Countersink the nails and fill the nail holes with wood putty. Turn the unit over and repeat the same steps for the other side.

The back pieces consist of two back rails and a back trim. Attach the trim by gluing and nailing it across the back so the top is even with the top of the sides. To reinforce the shelves, glue and nail the rails vertically along their back edges (see Fig. 2-105). When the glue has dried, sand the outside edges of the rails so they are flush with the sides. Also round off the top front edges of the sides and sand smooth.

The drawers are made with simple lap joints (see pages 29–31) except for the ¼-inch by ¼-inch dadoes on their interior to accept the ¼-inch-thick masonite bottoms. For the specific dimensions of these drawers, refer to Fig. 2-103. They also use 10-inch metal telescoping drawer slides. Remember to leave ½-inch clearance between the drawer and the side unit to allow for the thickness of these telescoping slides.

Cover the front edges of the plywood shelves with wood veneer edging tape (see Fig. 1-29, page 35) and finish with either three coats of polyurethane or enamel paint.

After installing your equipment in the appropriate compartments and connecting the wires through the open back of the unit, check to make sure everything works correctly. We found it very helpful to label each wire and its connection with the same color of tape. This makes life easier if you have to move the unit to a new location.

To give the storage center even more stability, we recommend boring two ⅜-inch holes through the rear rails to attach it to the wall with large washers and molly bolts. Note that the back rails stop 5½ inches above the floor in order to allow space for the baseboard.

DESIGN IDEAS & INSPIRATIONS

T HE FOLLOWING DESIGN IDEAS DO NOT INCLUDE PLANS OR DIRECTIONS but are provided simply to help inspire you to design your own children's furniture. For readers who have some building expertise, this section can be a first step toward planning an original design for your child's room.

HOBBY WORK AREA

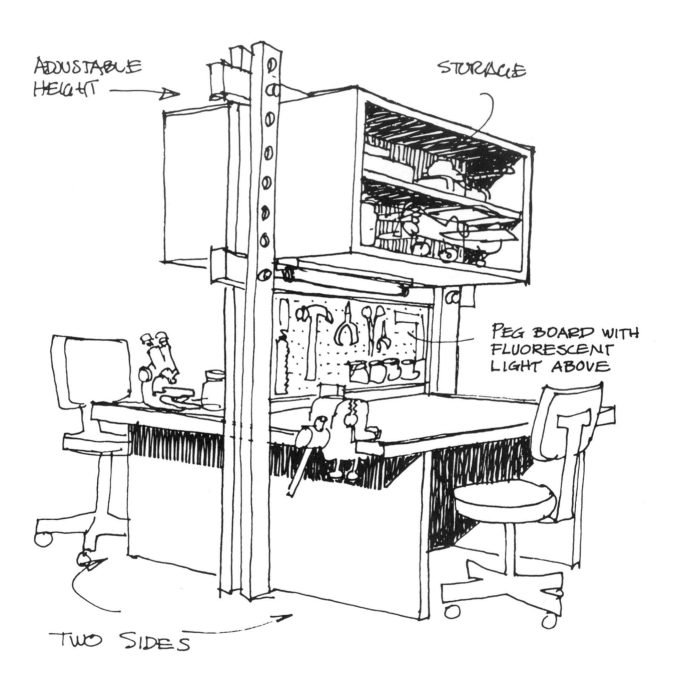

ADJUSTABLE HEIGHT

STORAGE

PEG BOARD WITH FLUORESCENT LIGHT ABOVE

TWO SIDES

GIRL'S DRESSER AND DESK #1

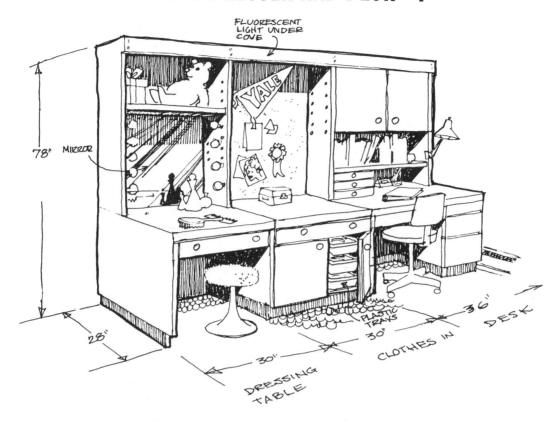

GIRL'S DRESSER AND DESK #2

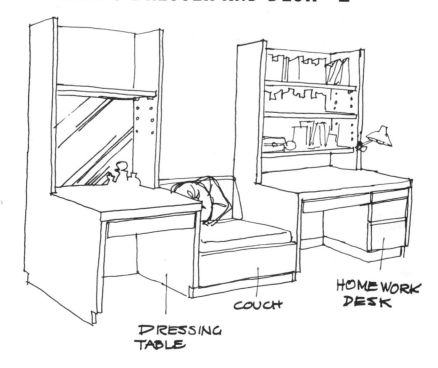

TEENAGER'S HABITAT CUBE

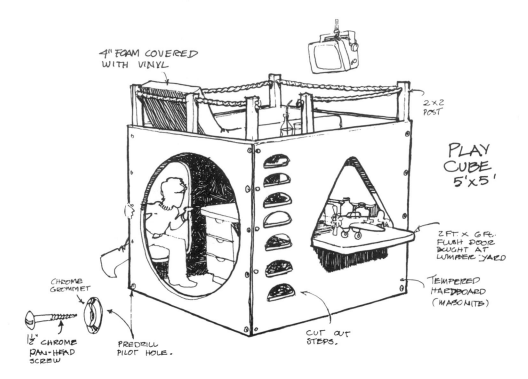

4" FOAM COVERED WITH VINYL

2x2 POST

PLAY CUBE 5'x5'

2 FT. X 6 FT. FLUSH DOOR BOUGHT AT LUMBER YARD

TEMPERED HARDBOARD (MASONITE)

CHROME GROMMET

1½" CHROME PAN-HEAD SCREW

PREDRILL PILOT HOLE.

CUT OUT STEPS.

BUNK BEDS, DESK AND DRESSER

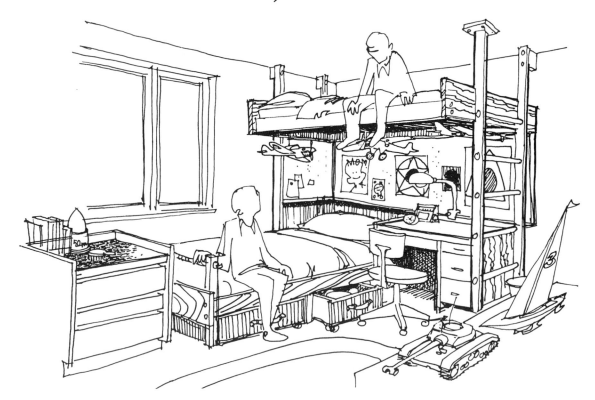

House Bed with Playhouse Above

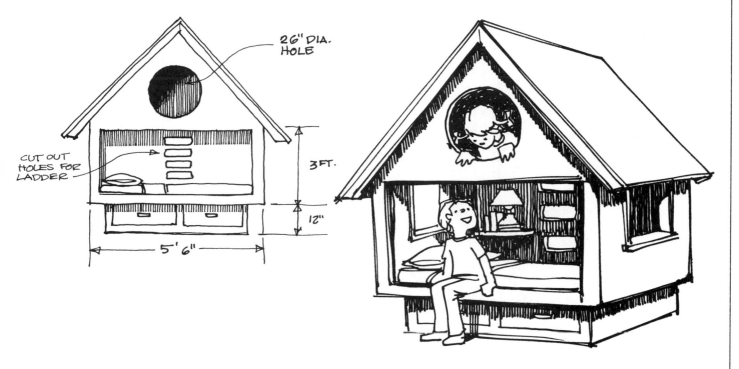

26" DIA. HOLE

CUT OUT HOLES FOR LADDER

3 FT.

12"

5' 6"

Cabinets

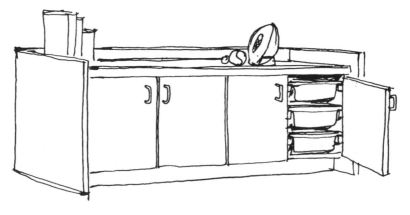

MODEL RAILROAD WALL UNIT

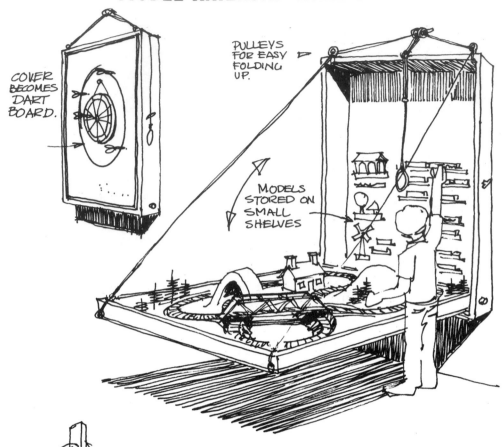

COVER BECOMES DART BOARD.

PULLEYS FOR EASY FOLDING UP.

MODELS STORED ON SMALL SHELVES

READING ROOM

DON'T LOOK

8 FT.

5 FT.

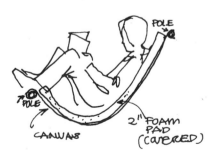

POLE

POLE

CANVAS

2" FOAM PAD (COVERED)

Built-in Desk

Built-in Beds and Storage

EAVES STORAGE

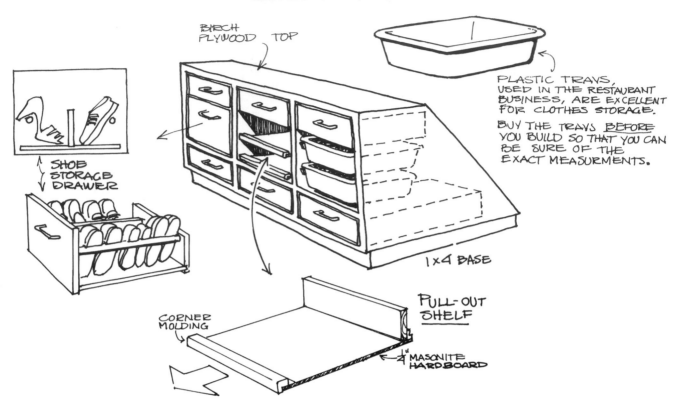

BIRCH PLYWOOD TOP

PLASTIC TRAYS, USED IN THE RESTAURANT BUSINESS, ARE EXCELLENT FOR CLOTHES STORAGE.

BUY THE TRAYS _BEFORE_ YOU BUILD SO THAT YOU CAN BE SURE OF THE EXACT MEASURMENTS.

SHOE STORAGE DRAWER

1×4 BASE

CORNER MOLDING

PULL-OUT SHELF

¼" MASONITE HARDBOARD

CLOTHES STORAGE

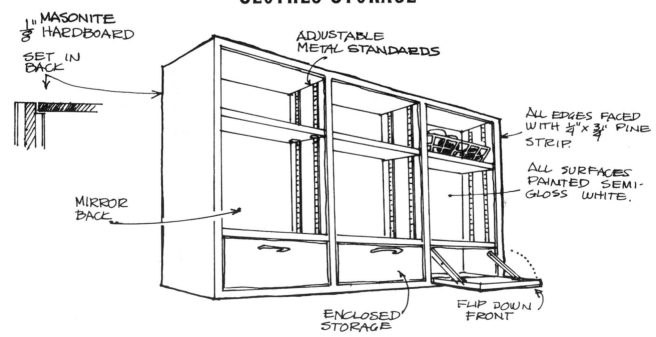

⅛" MASONITE HARDBOARD

SET IN BACK

ADJUSTABLE METAL STANDARDS

ALL EDGES FACED WITH ¼" × ¾" PINE STRIP.

ALL SURFACES PAINTED SEMI-GLOSS WHITE.

MIRROR BACK

ENCLOSED STORAGE

FLIP DOWN FRONT

WALL DESK-AREA SPACE SAVER

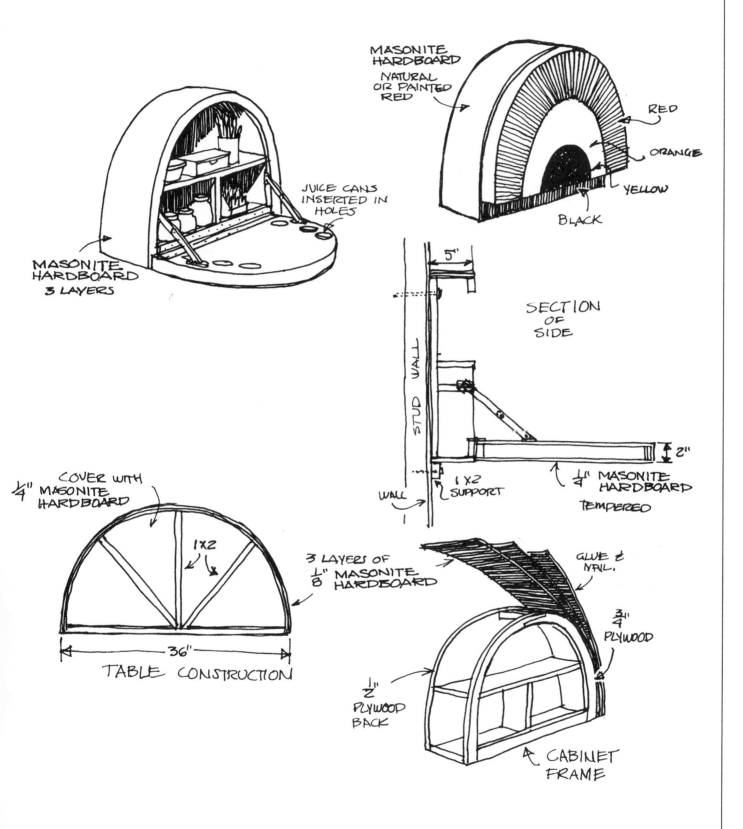

MASONITE
HARDBOARD
3 LAYERS

MASONITE
HARDBOARD
NATURAL
OR PAINTED
RED

JUICE CANS
INSERTED IN
HOLES

RED
ORANGE
YELLOW
BLACK

SECTION
OF
SIDE

STUD WALL

WALL

5"

1 X 2
SUPPORT

2"

$\frac{1}{4}$" MASONITE
HARDBOARD
TEMPERED

COVER WITH
$\frac{1}{4}$" MASONITE
HARDBOARD

1 X 2

36"

TABLE CONSTRUCTION

3 LAYERS OF
$\frac{1}{8}$" MASONITE
HARDBOARD

GLUE &
NAIL

$\frac{3}{4}$"
PLYWOOD

$\frac{1}{2}$"
PLYWOOD
BACK

CABINET
FRAME

TWO-PIECE TOY STORAGE

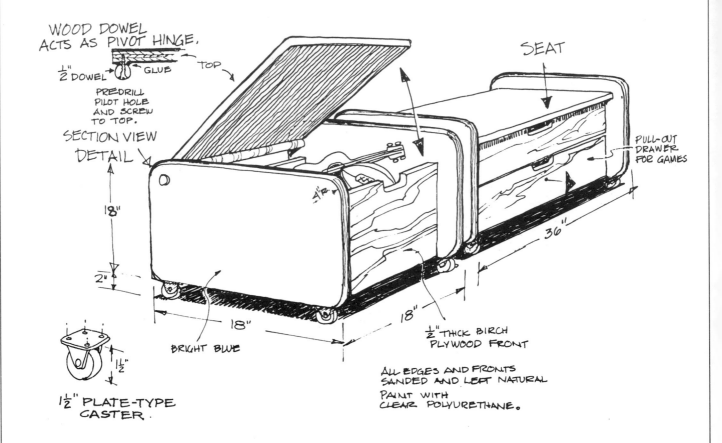

WOOD DOWEL ACTS AS PIVOT HINGE.

$\frac{1}{2}$" DOWEL GLUE TOP

PREDRILL PILOT HOLE AND SCREW TO TOP.

SECTION VIEW DETAIL

18"

2"

$1\frac{1}{2}$"

$1\frac{1}{2}$" PLATE-TYPE CASTER.

BRIGHT BLUE

18"

SEAT

PULL-OUT DRAWER FOR GAMES

36"

18"

$\frac{1}{2}$" THICK BIRCH PLYWOOD FRONT

ALL EDGES AND FRONTS SANDED AND LEFT NATURAL

PAINT WITH CLEAR POLYURETHANE.

SOURCES

TOOLS AND HARDWARE

SEARS POWER AND HAND TOOLS
20 Presidential Dr.
Roselle, IL 60172

GARRETT WADE
302 Fifth Ave
New York, NY 10001

HARBOR FREIGHT
3491 Mission Oaks Blvd.
Camarillo, CA 93011

TRENDLINES
375 Beacham St.
Chelsea, MA 02150

THE WOODWORKERS' STORE
21801 Industrial Blvd.
Rogers, MN 55374-9514

GENERAL HARDWARE

MCFEELY'S
712 Twelfth St.
P.O. Box 3
Lynchburg, VA 24505-0003

MARINE HARDWARE

DEFENDER'S INDUSTRIES, INC.
225 Main St.
P.O. Box 820
New Rochelle, NY 10801-0820

ABOUT THE AUTHORS

RICHARD D'ALONZO

DAVID STILES is a designer/builder and the author of seven
other how-to books, including *Sheds*, *The Treehouse Book* (which won the
ALA Notable Children's Book Award) and *Playhouses You Can Build*.
A graduate of Pratt Institute and The Academy of Fine Arts in
Florence, Italy, he is the winner of two awards from the New York
Planning Commission for his designs for "The Playground
for All Children." His articles have appeared in *House Beautiful*,
Popular Mechanics, *American Home* and the *New York Times*.

JEAN TRUSTY STILES, a graduate of Wheaton College, lives in New York
City, where she is an actress/model and an instructor of English as a
Second Language at Baruch College. Jeanie and David have a twenty-
year-old daughter, Lief-Anne, who is a student at Duke University.
They divide their time between New York City and East Hampton.